Formed in the Word

Lessons for Gospel Living

Formed in the Word

Lessons for Gospel Living

Patricia Datchuck Sánchez

Sheed & Ward
Kansas City

Sheed & Ward™ is a service of The National Catholic
Reporter Publishing Company.

Library of Congress Cataloguing-in-Publication Data
Sánchez, Patricia Datchuck.
    Formed in the Word : lessons for Gospel living /
Patricia Datchuck Sánchez.
        p.   cm.
    ISBN: 1-55612-923-8
    1. Christian life—Biblical teaching. 2. Bible—Criticism,
interpretation, etc. 3. Spiritual life—Catholic Church.
4. Catholic Church—Doctrines. 5. Sánchez, Patricia
Datchuck.   I. Title.
BS680.C47S26 1997
242—dc21   97-17876
                                                            CIP

Published by: Sheed & Ward
                115 E. Armour Blvd.
                P.O. Box 419492
                Kansas City, MO 64141-6492

To order, call: (800) 333-7373

www.natcath.com/sheedward

Contents

Prophecy

Reconciliation

To:

L.L. Terstroet, S.M.M.
and
R.E. Brown, S.S.
Through whom I was first introduced to the Word

and

To:

Rafael Sánchez Alonso, my husband and best
friend, without whom none of this would have
been possible and with whom it continues to be a
labor of love.

The Beatitudes

Portrait of a
New Social Order

Chapter One

A New Social Order

In Jesus' day, one of the questions most frequently posed to rabbis, priests or scribes was a request for a summary of the law. An immense compendium based on the decalogue, or ten commandments, over the centuries the law had evolved into a composite of written as well as oral prescriptions, intended to govern and guide every possible thought, word and deed of Jewish life.

When queried on the topic, legal experts would quote what they had determined to be the linchpin, which succinctly stated the law, and upon which the

> Do justice, love tenderly, walk humbly with God.

rest of the law hung. One popular rabbi, Hillel, gave this response, "What you hate for yourself, do not do to your neighbor. This is the whole law, the rest is commentary. Go and learn." Another rabbi, Sammlai, taught that Moses had received 613 precepts on Mt. Sinai, 365 according to the days of the year and 248 according to the generations of men. During his reign, David was purported to have reduced the 613 precepts to the 11 rules of behavior prescribed in Psalm 15. Isaiah went even further and reduced the law to six statutes (Isaiah 33:15). Micah, an eighth-century B.C.E. prophet and a contemrary of First Isaiah, gave what is perhaps the most beautiful and poignant summary of the law in all of the Jewish scriptures: "God has shown you, what is good and what is required of you . . . Only this – to do justice, to love tenderly and to walk humbly with your God!" (Micah 6:8).

When his first-century contemporaries challenged him with the summary of the law, Jesus responded by putting the love of one's neighbor on a par with loving God with one's whole heart, soul, mind and strength. But Jesus was more than a law-giver; he was the proclaimer of a new era. Indeed, the very essence of Jesus' message and mission was the proclamation of the reign of God. Whereas his fellow Jews were anticipating a messiah and a royal reign which they perceived in earthly, political and socioeconomic terms, Jesus came proclaiming a reign of vastly different dimensions. Jesus proclaimed that the reign of God had become present by virtue of his mission and his message (Mark 1:15, Matthew 4:17). He made it clear that this reign was not merely an earthly territory, however majestic and powerful, but rather the very presence, in time and space, of the saving activity of God. Because of the eruption of that reign in the appearance of Jesus, an entirely new social order was called for.

> **THE REIGN OF GOD demands a new morality, a new ethic of behavior.**

In his inaugural address, Jesus set forth the characteristics of that new social order. "The spirit of the Lord is upon me . . . He has sent me to bring good news to the poor, to proclaim freedom to captives, recovery of sight to the blind and release to prisoners . . . " (Luke 4:18-19). Most of Jesus' contemporaries regarded the poor, the captives, the blind and otherwise physically handicapped as sinners, whose malady was a deserved punishment for sin. And while his contemporaries had come to view their own sharing in the reign of God, i.e., salvation, as Israel's deserved reward for their obedient observance of the law and avoidance of sin, Jesus offered an entirely different view of salvation, as the undeserved, unmerited, gracious gift of God to each and every sinful human being. Having turned their centuries' old notions of God's reign and of salvation upside down, Jesus then proceeded to challenge his contemporaries to embrace a new morality . . . a new ethic of behavior that went beyond the limits of the Mosaic law. Indeed, he called them, and us, to a perfection motivated not by legalism but by love, and to a way of life inspired and catalyzed by the loving relationship to which God invites every sinner.

Each of the four evangelists has preserved the challenges Jesus proffered to believers in the gospels they have handed on to us. Matthew and Luke distilled these challenges and Jesus' call for a new social order in their respective versions of the Great Sermon (Matthew 5:1-7:29, Luke 6:17-49). Unfortunately, many believers read the Great Sermon and find its demands too difficult and even unrealistic. Some think Jesus was enunciating an ideal that is unattainable in this life. Martin Luther called the Great Sermon "a pernicious document which has wrought incalculable harm by presenting an utterly impossible ethic." Others have described the Great Sermon as an interim ethic the demands of which could be satisfied, but only for a short period of time, as in a "last-ditch" effort at preparing for death or for the second advent of Jesus. Perhaps this negativism springs from a continuing misconception of God's reign and of salvation. For those who persist in regarding the experience of the reign and of salvation as a prize they can merit, and who look only to their own resources for their strength and sustenance, the demands of the Great Sermon appear too costly. But for those who draw their strength from the reign of God, i.e., the saving activity of God present among us, the challenge of the Great Sermon can be met. Reliant on God, on God's power and on the grace of divine provenance, the Sermon becomes a realistic, albeit challenging, description of life in Christ.

Significantly, both versions of Jesus' Great Sermon begin with the catalogue of blessings we have come to call "The Beatitudes." With each shocking pronouncement of those who are blessed, viz., the poor, the mourning, the meek, the hungry, the merciful, the persecuted, etc., the parameters of the new social order are delineated, and the characteristics of those who will enjoy God's reign are defined. Moreover, the beatitudes describe that attitude of openness, acceptance, truthfulness and trust in God which make it possible to meet the challenges of the Great Sermon.

Reflections

1. Do you believe the demands of the Great Sermon to be realistic?

2. Can the demands be met in a civilization teetering on the brink of the third Christian millennium?

Chapter Two

Not Prerequisites But Dispositions

As if to summon their readers to strict attention, the evangelists often used literary signals to indicate the importance or seriousness of Jesus' teaching. Concerning the Beatitudes and the Great Sermon which they introduce, the signals are quite definitive. In the seemingly simple declaration, "Seeing the crowds, he went up on the mountain, and when he sat down, his disciples came to him. And he opened his mouth and taught them, saying . . . " (Matthew 5:1-2), Matthew has made it clear that what follows is a teaching of extreme moment for all believers.

As we carefully examine Matthew's literary signals, we see that he has located the site of the Beatitudes on a mountain. Matthew, who wrote his gospel for second and third-generation Christians in the 80s C.E., was intent upon showing Jesus as the fulfillment of all the prophecies and divine promises as recorded in the Hebrew Scriptures (Old Testament). For this reason, he cast Jesus as a New Moses, a new leader for a new Israel. As Moses had presented the decalogue centuries before on Mt. Sinai, Jesus was propounding the rules for those who would be members of the new people of God. It is interesting that Luke, who wrote his gospel about the same time as Matthew, situated Jesus and the crowds in a plain. Writing mainly for Gentile believers, Luke knew that the mountain would have had little significance for those unfamiliar with Jewish tradition.

Secondly, Matthew signaled his readers by deliberately pointing out Jesus' seated position. In the ancient world, this was the official posture for delivering an important teaching. Rabbis sat when elucidating for their students the mysteries of God's ways. In the synagogues, the layperson appointed to lead the Sabbath service would sit when expounding upon God's word. Recall the instance when Jesus led the service in his hometown of Nazareth, "And he closed the book and gave it back to the attendant and sat down; and the eyes of all in the synagogue were fixed on him. And he began to teach them . . . (Luke 4:20-21). Kings, queens, judges and governors also sat when delivering their judgments or proclaiming official decrees (John 19:13). Even today, this custom is preserved. When the pope renders an official statement, he is said to speak *ex cathedra*, i.e., from the chair or seat of papal authority. We refer to the center of government in a particular area as the *seat* of government or the county *seat*. So too, positions of authority at universities or even of committees are called *chairs*. Therefore it appears that Matthew intended to alert his readers to the fact that the seated Jesus was about to deliver an authoritative teaching.

A third signal included by the evangelist, and one not immediately obvious to the modern reader, is the statement, "He opened his mouth" (Matthew 5:2). While this may seem to be a contrived way of explaining that Jesus spoke to the crowds, it was nevertheless a signal that was clear to first-century believers. The statement, "He opened his mouth," indicated that a very profound and significant message was to be delivered. When kings of the ancient world delivered official edicts, they were said to have opened their mouths. In the Christian Scriptures (New Testament), Luke used this term two times, and in each case it referred to the official declaration of the good news of salvation (Acts 8:35; 10:34). In addition to signaling an important utterance, "He opened his mouth" was also used of a declaration which required great courage. Regardless of the consequences which might be incurred, the speaker who opened his/her mouth said what needed to be said.

Finally, the statement "He opened his mouth" indicated that the speaker spoke with an open heart, and with no reservations told the whole truth. In Aeschylus' *Prometheus Vinctus*, the character was said to have opened his mouth, telling all – as one would speak to friends. By means of this simple phrase, "He opened his mouth," Matthew explained that Jesus' words were of great significance and that, in them, he divulged his very heart and mind to his hearers, thinking not of himself, but only of them and the message he wished them to receive.

That this particular event of teaching on the mountain was not a unique occurrence, but was rather a habitual practice of Jesus, is communicated in the special verb tense employed by the evangelist. In Greek, there are two tenses for describing past actions, the aorist and the imperfect. While the aorist tense indicates one particular act, done and completed in the past, the imperfect tense describes a repeated, continuous or habitual action. By using the imperfect tense, Matthew was, in effect, telling his readers that this was the manner in which Jesus customarily taught and this was the message he continuously communicated. Therefore the message of the beatitudes represents a *summary* or a *distillation* of the teaching which Jesus *consistently* shared with his disciples.

> **THE bEATiTUdES ARE NOT pREREQUiSiTES bUT THE RESUlTiNq dispOSiTiONS of THOSE WHO ACCEpT God'S REiqN.**

Note well that, although crowds of people were present on the mountain, Matthew and Luke both made it clear that Jesus addressed the challenge of the beatitudes to *his disciples* (Matthew 5:1, Luke 6:17). These disciples or followers were those who had already opted for Jesus and had *faith* in him, however weak or wavering that faith may have been. Their faith commitment meant that grace was available to them. Indeed, the beatitudes *presuppose* grace; only then can Jesus' challenges be approached and embraced. Too many people regard the beatitudes as *requisites* for God's kingdom. The beatitudes are rather the *resulting* dispositions, deeds and decisions of those who have *already* held out their hands and hearts to accept and appropriate the reign of God in their own lives. Other people regard the beatitudes as eight separate entities descriptive of eight different kinds of character. Actually the beatitudes represent one character in eight different ways; the character described is remarkably like Jesus.

> **IN THE bEATiTUdES JESUS fRAMEd A vERbAl SElf-pORTRAiT.**

In other words, through the eight pronouncements of the beatitudes, Jesus created a type of verbal self-portrait, and in so doing, he invited those who believed in him to become like him, so as to fully experience the reign of God as he did.

Reflections

1. What are some of the literary signals by which Matthew alerted his readers to the importance of Jesus' teaching?

2. To whom were the beatitudes directed?

3. What enables believers to embrace and live the challenge of the beatitudes?

CHAPTER THREE

Blessed the Poor and Sorrowful

In the early 17th century, the spanish author Miguel de Cervantes wrote, in what was to become a world-renowned literary classic, "There are only two families in the world, the Have's and the Have Not's." (*Don Quixote* II). In our own century, the American playwright, Eugene O'Neill, declared of one of his characters, "The child was diseased at birth, stricken with a hereditary ill that only the most vital men are able to shake off. I mean poverty – the most deadly and prevalent of all diseases" (from O'Neill's play, *Fog*). Poverty, or being poor, has never been popular; indeed in Jesus' day, many of his contemporaries regarded the poor as sinners whose condition was a deserved punishment from God. Popular opinion notwithstanding, Jesus pronounced the poor as blessed.

In Greek, the word "blessed" or *makarios* referred to that perfect, God-given serenity which nothing can ruffle or diminish. Ancient Greeks referred to the island of Cyprus as *He Makaria*, or The Blessed Isle, because it provided its inhabitants with every needed and desired resource. So rich and abun-

> Blessedness is that perfect, God-given serenity which nothing can ruffle or diminish.

dant was the island in this world's goods that no one needed to look beyond its shores for complete fulfillment.

When Jesus applied this term "blessed" to those who would believe in him, he was, in effect, predicating of them that bliss which comes from sharing in the very life of God. Like the ancient inhabitants of Cyprus, those so blessed would never have to look elsewhere for their happiness!

While our English translations render the beatitudes as "Blessed are . . . " or "Happy are . . . ," the actual Greek and/or Hebrew texts contain no verbs. Therefore the beatitudes aren't simple declarative statements; they are more properly understood as exclamations, and could be rendered, "O, the blessedness of the person who . . ." (as in Psalms 1:1; 32:2; 94:12).

Some scholars have offered the suggestion that the beatitudes are to be understood as congratulatory expressions as in: "Congratulations you poor, you who mourn . . . !," etc. Moreover, each of the beatitudes should be understood not only as promises of *future* happiness; they are, rather, affirmations of *present* joy. As William Barclay has noted, "this is not to say that this bliss will not be perfected at the consummation of the reign of God, but even here and now, the taste of that bliss is meant to be part of the Christian experience."

> THE bEATITUdES ARE NOT ONLY PROMISES Of fUTURE HAppiNESS; THEY ARE AffiRMATIONS Of PRESENT joy.

At the top of Jesus' roster of blessedness are the poor. In Greek there were two terms for the poor: *Penes* described those who must work for a living; this would apply to all but the independently wealthy! *Ptochos*, on the other hand, referred to those who were absolutely destitute. It is significant that in both Matthew 5:3 and Luke 6:20, the word used is *ptochos*! Whereas the Lucan beatitude designated the materially poor as blessed, the Matthean beatitude has been expanded by the addition of "in spirit." By virtue of this expansion, Matthew associated the "poor in spirit" of Jesus' beatitude to the *anawim* or "poor ones."

As Albert Gelin has pointed out in his book, *The Poor of Yahweh*, the term *anawim* underwent a gradual evolution in the Hebrew Scriptures. Initially it simply designated the materially poor. Then it came to refer to those with no power, prestige or influence (as in the case of widows, orphans and exiles). Eventually, *anawim* came also to mean the downtrodden and oppressed. Finally, a spirituality evolved such that the *anawim,* or poor ones, were those who found their sole source of security, trust and riches in God and who were reliant upon divine providence for everything. Keenly aware of their finitude and deep spiritual inadequacies, the fidelity of the poor ones contrasted sharply with the rich, whose wealth, power and self-sufficiency had dulled their sense of the sacred and silenced their longings for God.

When Jesus pronounced the poor ones as "Blessed the poor ones," his words also offered an invitation to the materially rich. One of the most heartrending stories ever written is that of the young man who was sent sadly away from Jesus because his possessions were many (Mark 10:22 and parallels). But Jesus' words are also to be understood as a challenge to those whose prejudices and expectations prevent them from recognizing the truth of his mission and his messiahship. As Emmet Fox has observed, the poor of the first beatitude are those who have "emptied themselves of self-will and renounced all preconceived opinions in the wholehearted search for God." These blessed poor are those who are "willing to set aside present habits of thought, present views and even their present way of life, if necessary, for God. Once every other source of security has been jettisoned, the poor one is free for the full experience of God and of salvation." Jesus called that experience the kingdom or reign of God. He also assured his followers that those who were willing to value the full experience of God above all other things would not be left in abject need; on the contrary, Jesus declared, "Seek *first* God's reign over you, God's way of holiness, and *all things* will be given you besides" (Matthew 6:33).

Second on Jesus' roster of blessedness are the mourning or the sorrowing. In Greek, the word used is the strongest term for mourning; it pertains to the deepest grief one can experience, viz., the grief for the loss of a dearly loved one. The same term was used in the *LXX* (Greek translation of the Hebrew Scriptures) to describe the anguished mourning of Jacob when told of Joseph's supposed death (Genesis 37:34).

Deep sorrow can have a variety of effects. Some people respond to sorrow with an angry bitterness that shrivels their abilities to grow, to love, to relate to others. In the end, that bitterness creates an isolation that stifles and eventually kills. For others, deep sorrow or mourning can become an impetus for discovery. "Sorrow can show us," says William Barclay, "as nothing else can, the essential kindness of our fellow men and it can show us as nothing else can the comfort and compassion of God." Many of us are reluctant to enter into this process of discovery until we are forced into it by some personal tragedy. Some of us resort to God only when all our other resources have failed. How often have you heard, "Well, all we can do now is pray!"? Jesus' second beatitude challenges us to become aware of the fact that believers are to be a people in mourning . . . not a maudlin melancholy but a deep sense of sorrow at the fact of sin and at the grave losses which sin effects. Sin's death toll is a stark reality; sin alienates us from God, from one another and even from our own hopes and ideals. Believers are called to a vivid awareness of these losses and to a mourning which impels them to seek out God and one another with a repentant heart. Jesus' promised reward for those who would so mourn is comfort. Etymologically, comfort means to make strong; therefore, while believers in Jesus aren't immune to sin or its ravages, we are, because of Jesus, strengthened for the confrontation. We are, in a word, blessed!

Reflections

1. Describe the character and attitude of the poor ones or *anawim* whom Jesus pronounced as blessed.
2. Why did Jesus declare as blessed those who mourn and have sorrow?
3. What are some of the possible responses to sorrow?

Chapter Four

Blessed the Meek and Hungry

"Blessed are the meek; they shall inherit the earth."

Not many of us would be flattered if another person referred to us as "meek." In today's usage, meekness conjures up images of Caspar Milquetoast, a spineless and timid comic strip character created by H.T. Webster. Because we tend to equate meekness with weakness and subservience, we lose the truly powerful meaning of this beatitude. Even "lowly," as some translations render the word, fails to communicate the challenge intended by Jesus.

In Jewish tradition, the poor ones, or *anawim*, were considered meek, i.e., they had the strength and courage to seek for God even in seemingly impossible circumstances. Their reliance on God was the source of their strength; therefore the meek were not considered weak, but invincible.

> **Meekness is not weakness but strength, courage, self-control and God-control.**

In Greek (the language in which Matthew and Luke expressed the beatitudes) the term for "meek" is *praus*, one of the great ethical concepts. Aristotle taught extensively about the virtue of meekness (*praotes*), and his insights are helpful in grasping what the term meant for Jesus and for the evangelists.

Because the ancients methodically defined virtue as the mean between two extremes, meekness was understood as the mean between too much and too little anger. Anger was regarded as a strong medicine which, when used justifiably and in a controlled manner, can bring about great good, but when used in a selfish, resentful or destructive way, anger was thought to be a poison that can kill.

Meekness also had other meanings as well for Jesus' contemporaries. For example, an animal that had been domesticated and/or trained to carry out commands was called meek. When applied to humanity, this notion of meekness described the person who was capable of control, i.e., self-control, as well as that "God-control" which comes from accepting the will of God in one's life. In that acceptance comes perfect freedom, fulfillment and peace. The term "meek" was also predicated of the person who has the capacity to act with severity but chooses to act with gentleness. Great rulers of the ancient world had it in their power to behave as tyrants; those who chose to exercise kindness were praised as meek.

When Jesus challenged believers to that quality of meekness which manifested itself in self-control, gentleness and strength, he also promised that those meek would inherit the earth! The Jews among Jesus' contemporaries would have recognized this beatitude as a direct quote from Psalm 37:11, wherein the meek of Israel were assured of a place on earth to call their own, viz., the promised land. But for believers in Jesus, the inheritance means more than a portion of real estate. As Emmet Fox has observed in his excellent book, *Sermon on the Mount*, "earth" means the whole of one's outer experience. To inherit the earth means to "have dominion over that outer experience . . . to have the power to bring all aspects of one's life into harmony." In more colloquial terms, those who have learned meekness might be inclined to declare, "the world is my *oyster!*" because through their meekness they have been able to recognize and enjoy the *pearl* (pun intended) of great price, i.e., the reign of God.

Matthew's fourth beatitude presents modern believers with an experience most can only imagine: "Blessed are those who hunger and thirst for righteousness; they shall have their fill." Few of us have ever been hungry or thirsty to the degree implied in this beatitude. The hunger herein portrayed is that of a starving person, for whom a bit of bread means the difference between life and death. The thirst herein portrayed is that of a person whose parched body is choking for relief. But the sustenance longed for in this beatitude is not bread and water; rather, the hungry and thirsty pronounced blessed by Jesus are those whose appetites are ravenous for righteousness!

> **RiqHTEOUSNESS MEANS TO livE wHolE ANd holy bEfoRE God ANd oTHER pEoplE.**

Righteousness, a key concept of the Bible, mentioned over 500 times in the Hebrew Scriptures and over 225 times in the Christian Scriptures, means the state of being integral or whole and holy in God's eyes. To attain this integrity or justice, the righteous person thinks rightly, speaks rightly, acts rightly, loves rightly, etc. Jews believed that such righteousness was achieved by observing the law. When Jesus came, he called for a *higher* righteousness that *presumed* the law and went far beyond it. Jesus' higher righteousness could only be reached by those who accepted not the law as their norm, but his very person in all his words and works. In a word, then, Jesus' beatitude challenges believers to so desire wholeness and holiness in such a powerful and instinctive way that without it they would perish.

Included also in this beatitude is a social sense of hungering and thirsting for wholeness and justice for *others*, especially those who are victims of injustice. When this Matthean beatitude is compared with that of Luke, the gospel reader will discover that Luke included an admonition. "Blessed are you that hunger now, for you shall be filled" (Luke 6:21) has been complemented by "Woe to you who are full, for you shall hunger!" (Luke 6:25). While most of us have never experienced the degree of hunger described in the beatitude, we have probably known the type of fullness or self-satisfaction against which Luke warns. As William Barclay has noted, "Most people have a desire for goodness (a hunger for righteousness), but when the moment of decision comes, they are not prepared to make the effort and the sacrifice which real goodness demands." They are, as it were, satisfied with the *status quo*. In his book, *The Master of Ballantrae*, Robert Louis Stevenson described this satiety as "the malady of not wanting." This state of "not-wanting" or that fullness that keeps us from risking all for the sake of goodness is an ever-present danger. Contentment with self dulls the hunger that should characterize the Christian.

Significantly, Jesus' promise to all those who hunger and thirst for righteousness is that they will *be filled*. Filled, or *chortazesthai* in Greek, was a term ordinarily used to describe the coddling, pampering and fattening of animals which were raised for their meat. In the gospel context, as applied to human beings, the word means that the believer is filled, not with self, but with God, and in that wonderful condition has no further experience of need, desire or longing of any kind. Only the truly hungry and thirsty can ever hope to experience this blessed fullness!

Reflections:

1. What are the hungers that motivate you to action?
2. How can these hungers be satisfied?
3. What danger is there in being full and/or satisfied?

Chapter Five

Blessed the Merciful and the Pure

"Blessed are the merciful; they shall know mercy" (Matthew 5:7). Over three centuries ago, the famous bard of Stratford-on-Avon eulogized mercy in this way: "The quality of mercy is not strained; it droppeth as the gentle rain from heaven upon the place beneath. It is twice blest; it blesseth him that gives and him that takes. 'Tis mightiest in the mightiest; it becomes the throned monarch better than his crown." Many who cite this quote from Shakespeare's play, *Merchant of Venice* (Act IV, scene 1), end the citation at this point; but the bard continued, adding ". . . and earthly power doth then show likest God's, when mercy seasons justice." Shakespeare understood that mercy was not a human invention, but a divine quality; this fact lies at the heart of Jesus' fifth beatitude.

Whereas we tend to define mercy in a rather limited sense, as "clemency," or as "the alleviation of distress," or as the "relaxing of a demand which may have been severely enforced," the scriptural notion of mercy is much more comprehensive. Appearing in more than 150 texts in the Hebrew Scriptures and 27 times in the Christian Scriptures, the terms for mercy (Hebrew: *chesedh*; Greek: *eleos*) are applied to God in more than 90% of these occurrences. Defined as loving-kindness or outgoing compassion, *chesedh* or mercy is regarded as belonging properly to God (Isaiah 62:12), and as an infinite quality that endures forever (Psalms 36:5; 57:10; 89:1-2; 100:5;

103:17; 106:1; 107:1; 136; 138:8; 1 Chronicles 16:34; 2 Chronicles 7:3; Ezra 3:11; Jeremiah 33:11).

Israel believed that the mercy of God had become visible and palpable in nature (Psalm 119:64; Job 37:13) and in human history. For example, in the exodus from Egypt (Exodus 15:13), the mercy of God translated itself into freedom and nationhood for a motley band of refugees. In the return from exile (Ezra 9:9), the mercy of God made itself felt in terms of forgiveness, restoration and a new beginning. That mercy, which has its origin in God, is the ground of human hope (Psalms 33:18; 51:13; 59:10; 90:14) and the reason for human strength and joy, even in the midst of great suffering and/or difficulties (Psalms 31:7; 94:18).

Since mercy is the basic characteristic of God's relationship with humankind, mercy must also be the basis for all interpersonal human relationships. More than pity or sympathy, the quality of divine mercy, as elucidated in the Scriptures, means getting inside another's skin until we see with his/her eyes and think with his/her thoughts and feel with his/her feelings. Mercy, in the scriptural sense, means knowing another person as she knows herself so that we truly might understand and love that person. Isn't this precisely what God did for us in Jesus? By virtue of the incarnation and in the most literal sense, God "got inside the skin" of humanity; God took on the flesh of humanity so as to see with human eyes, think with a human mind and feel with a human heart. In Jesus, God has fully communicated the gift of mercy to us in our own language, i.e., the lan-

> The merciful see others with the eyes of God.

guage of our own flesh and blood and day-to-day existence.

Since as believers we profess to hear, to know and to live according to the gift of God's mercy, who is Jesus, then we are to reproduce in our own lives that same mercy. To live God's mercy, or to be merciful, is to have the same attitude toward one another as God has. It is to look at others and to see them with the same magnanimous vision that God has. Mercy is primarily outgoing. As William Barclay has noted, "Mercy is the reverse of self-centeredness . . . it is the attitude of the person for whom the needs of others are more important than his own and the sorrows of others are more poignant than his own." But this mercy is not possible for those who persist, either consciously or unconsciously, in regarding themselves as the center of the universe.

Mercy comes to life when outgoing and other-centered love is actualized. It isn't simply emotion; mercy is also action. In the Christian Scriptures we do not simply read, "God so loved the world"; rather we read, "God so loved the world *that he gave his only Son*" (John 3:16). We also read, "Jesus emptied himself and took on the form of a slave . . . " (Philippians 2:7). The mercy of God and the mercy of Jesus, and therefore the mercy of humanity, must of its very nature issue forth in altruistic love, care, forgiveness and service.

In order to be authentic, mercy must happen from the inside out; truly merciful deeds are first motivated by a merciful heart and mind. While an action may be kind, unless it is motivated by kind thoughts, it is hypocrisy. There is also an element of *freedom* in true mercy. Mercy frees the one who has sinned to do what is right; mercy does not shackle others with the burden of our condemnation; mercy frees others for repentance and the experience of forgiveness.

Most of all, mercy expects the best of others; mercy believes in the possibility of growth and change, even radical change in even the most seemingly unchangeable people. Because of this quality, mercy empowers the person to be different . . . to change . . . to become better . . . to become the best they can be. As Jesus has promised, for all those who have learned mercy at God's hand and exercise that mercy with others, *there shall be mercy.*

"Blessed are the pure in heart; they shall see God" (Matthew 5:8). So goes the sixth challenge of the beatitudes. Pure, or *katharos* in Greek, is a term with a wide range of meaning. For example, clean, unsoiled clothes are considered *katharos* or pure. All things which are unalloyed and unadulterated by foreign materials, e.g., milk, wine, water, silver, gold, are termed pure. So too, purity is a quality predicated of unblemished animals. There were many other instances where the word *katharos* or pure was applied in the ancient world: it referred to winnowed grain with no trace of chaff, to an army with no defectors, to persons of pure blood lineage, to a language free of colloquialisms and errors of grammar, and to persons free of debt.

In the Hebrew Scriptures, the term "pure" has two distinct applications: it refers first to ceremonial or ritual purity as regards foods, animals, washing, etc., prescribed by law. This first application has little or nothing to do with moral integrity. In the second application, the term "pure" describes moral and spiritual purity.

From the gospels, we can determine that Jesus had little use for ceremony or ritualism. In fact, this beatitude specifies, "Blessed are the pure *in heart* . . . " Jesus further clarified his point in another text, "Nothing that enters a person from outside can make that person impure; that which comes out of the person, and only that, constitutes impurity" (Mark 7:15). Jesus challenges his followers to aspire to a purity that cannot be attained by any external laws, washing or rituals, however fastidiously these may be performed. Rather, Jesus calls for pure hearts, unalloyed by ulterior motives, unblemished by sin and unadulterated by hypocrisy.

Only clear-headed and honest self-examination can lead to purity of heart. But the self-examination of the believer does not focus solely inward upon the self. True self-examination focuses on *Christ* as the norm and ultimate *criterion*. Integral to such self-examination is

> THE PURE HEART BECOMES A WINDOW WHEREIN OTHERS CAN GLIMPSE THE GOODNESS OF God.

a willingness to enter a process of continual conversion . . . of turning away from self to Christ . . . away from sin to Christ. Within this dynamic of daily centering on and turning to Christ, believers receive the reward promised to the pure in heart – *they see God*, i.e., they enter here and now, into fuller knowledge of and communion with God. By virtue of the experience of seeing God, the believer's pure heart becomes a window, as it were, wherein others may glimpse the divine goodness and glory and be drawn nearer to God.

Reflections:

1. How is the quality of mercy a source of freedom?
2. How can purity of heart be learned?
3. Is there a difference between pity and mercy? Explain.

Chapter Six

Blessed the Peacemakers and the Persecuted

"Blessed are the peacemakers; they shall be called children of God" (Matthew 5:9). Without a doubt, the threat of impending conflict anywhere in the world causes most of the world's population to renew its efforts and desire for peace. But, even if every soldier were to complete their stint of military service without firing a shot, and even if all the implements for war

> **Making peace means working for the well-being of others.**

were disarmed and every plane were grounded, and even if the entire fleet of battleships were scuttled, the resulting situation would fall short of the biblical notion of peace.

Peace (*shalom* in Hebrew and *eirene* in Greek) is not merely the absence of war, nor can even the most finely negotiated truce be called peace in the biblical sense. Peace, according to the Scriptures, is a condition of positive and perfect well-being wherein there exists among all peoples right relationships, uninterrupted good will and a mutual respect that edifies or builds up each member individually and the community as a whole.

When Jesus pronounced this seventh beatitude, it is significant that he specified, "Blessed are the peace-*makers*." It is one thing to desire peace, or even to be able to *discuss* the terms of peace, and to *identify* what must occur in certain situations in order for peace to exist. It is quite another thing to have the intestinal fortitude to *do* something so as to *make* peace a *reality!*

Too frequently peace is equated with the impasse that results from evading the issues and avoiding conflict; but sometimes, in order to bring about a lasting peace, one must make trouble. True peace comes only when the issues are faced head-on. Often this type of unpopular confrontation includes suffering and difficulties. If we look at the gospels, we see that Jesus was often embroiled in head-on confrontations with the religious authorities of his day and even with his close friends and disciples. He did not avoid such situations. Jesus' commitment to God invited contradiction, even the ultimate contradiction, viz., his death on the cross. In him "we have peace with God" (Romans 5:1) because "he who is our peace has made us one by breaking down the barriers of hostility that kept us apart" (Ephesians 2:14).

When we, who profess faith in Jesus, put ourselves to the task of making peace, we frequently set our sights too high. Making peace will not require that we earn a degree in political science or pursue a career in diplomacy. Making peace will not require that we hone our skills at political negotiating or travel the globe to sit at a summit table. Making peace is possible right at our own dinner table, in our own neighborhood and within our own town. Making peace means working for the well-being of others. For the hungry, peace means food; for the thirsty, peace means a cup of cold water offered in Jesus' name. For the naked, peace means clothing; for the homeless, peace means a place to call home. For the sick, peace means the compassion of a caring hand; for the imprisoned, peace means a willing visitor. For the elderly, peace means being made to feel welcome and being valued as wise and worthwhile. For the estranged friend, relative or neighbor, peace means a renewed relationship. For the cranky or burdensome person, peace means patient acceptance. For the unemployed, peace means a job with a fair wage. For the unborn, peace means the right to be born and to enjoy the God-given gift of life. For the child, peace means a loving home and a family to love. For the person with AIDS, peace means freedom from the burden of society's condemnation and the support of compassionate friends. For the illiterate, peace means the chance to learn. For the person of color or the minority, peace means equal opportunity and respect. For the handicapped, peace means the right to develop as fully as possible. For the addict, peace means rehabilitation and a new beginning, unencumbered by criticism or suspicion.

In order to be a peacemaker in all of these situations, believers must learn to look at one another with the eyes and heart of God. When God looks at the created universe, those eyes are fully aware of human sin and infidelity, but God's heart does not condemn; when God looks at the world, those eyes do not see problems but possibilities! To learn to look at one another with the eyes and heart of God, we need only look to the person and message of Jesus; therein we shall find our vision, our energy and our resolve.

Before Jesus, who is our peace, left this earth, he bequeathed his peace to us. "Peace is my farewell to you, my peace is my gift to you (John 14:27). Our inheritance of this peace empowers us to be *makers* of peace, and in the process we realize the reward of the beatitude . . . we become children of God.

"Blessed are those who are persecuted for the sake of righteousness; theirs is the kingdom of heaven" (Matthew 5:10). As the first followers of Jesus stood in the shadow of his cross and reflected upon what life would thereafter be like for them, they had a sure certainty of at least one thing . . . the inevitability of suffering. As William Barclay has pointed out, one of the most illuminating facts about the language of the early Church is that before the end of the first Christian century, the word for a *witness* to Jesus Christ and the word for *martyr* had become the same Greek word!

> CHRISTIANS ARE CALLED TO A WAY OF LIFE THAT IS OFTEN "OUT-OF-SYNC" WITH THE WORLD.

By virtue of their witness to Christ, Christians were committed to a way of life that was "out of sync" or counter-culture with regard to the rest of society. Among their contemporaries, with their "eye for an eye and tooth for a tooth" (Exodus 21:24) brand of justice, Christians, with Jesus' mandate of loving enemies and turning the other cheek and forgiving the one who wrongs you seventy times seven times, stood out in stark contrast. Their differences and their beliefs made them suspect, unpopular and, eventually, the victims of persecution.

But those first followers of Jesus, who stood in the shadow of his cross and reflected upon what life would thereafter be like for them, were also assured of another great certainty! Jesus, who had come into the world to make palpable and visible the love and forgiveness of God for humankind, and who had suffered and died for the sake of that love and forgiveness, had also risen from the dead to life. Those who stand in the shadow of his cross will also stand in the glory of his resurrection. Both the shadow and the glory, both the suffering and the joy are part and parcel of the reign of God; this is the blessing and the challenge of the beatitudes.

Reflections:

1. What can peace mean to the poor, disadvantaged and disenfranchised of society?
2. What does peace mean to you?
3. Does your commitment to Christ ever bring suffering into your life?

Prayer

An Experience of the Compelling Presence of God

CHAPTER ONE

PRAYING AS AN ACTION-EVENT

Prayer and the experience of praying have been variously defined by both believers and skeptics for centuries. Thomas Szasz, a 20th-century Hungarian-born American psychiatrist once quipped, "If you talk to God, you are praying; if God talks to you, you have schizophrenia." In a more positive vein, Rabbi Abraham J. Heschel described prayer as a "humble answer to the inconceivable surprise of living." But, Heschel added, "In moments of crisis, a word of prayer is like a strap we take hold of when tottering in a rushing street car which seems

> MORE THAN THE RECITATION of CERTAIN WORd formulas, PRAYING IS AN ACTION-EVENT.

to be turning over." Scholar and minister, Robert McAfee Brown remarked that for many, "Prayer is like a foreign land. When we go there, we go as tourists. Like most tourists, we feel uncomfortable and out of place. Like most tourists, we therefore move on before long and go somewhere else." An ancient Arab proverb defined prayer as "the pillow of religion," whereas John O'Brien, a 20th-century Roman Catholic priest and author, once commented, "Like an opiate, sin drugs a conscience to drowsiness and stupor. Prayer stabs it wide awake!"

Whether at rest on a pillow or wide awake, prayer is an essential experience, without which the believer's relationship with God cannot develop and grow.

Christian believers have the decided advantage of a 3,000-year-old faith heritage through which to trace the roots of their experiences of praying. In both the Hebrew and Christian Scriptures, those who pray are represented as participating in a dynamic interchange with the living God. For this reason, perhaps it is appropriate to consider prayer, not as a static abstract noun but as an active, evolving gerund.

The *Webster's New World Guide to Current American Usage* (1988) defines a gerund as a verbal noun ending in "-ing." This reference work further explains, "Gerunds have all the uses of nouns but retain the characteristics of verbs." In other words, a gerund is an action-packed concept. In a very real sense, this definition approaches what is meant by the reality of Christian prayer. More than the recitation of certain words or formulas, praying is an action-event.

When the author of the book of Genesis first described the union between God and human beings in prayer, he spoke in terms of *walking* with God in the garden in the cool of the evening (Genesis 3:8). The psalmists sang of *shouting* to the Lord with joy (Psalm 33), of *rejoicing* in forgiveness (Psalm 32), of *blessing* of the Lord at all times (Psalm 34), of *resting* on green grass beside the cool water (Psalm 22), of *running* to God for shelter (Psalm 31), of *clapping* hands with joy for the Lord (Psalm 47), of *longing* for God like a deer longs for running streams (Psalm 42), of *celebrating* the love of God (Psalm 89), of *living* in the shelter of God's presence (Psalm 91), of *lifting* my eyes to the mountains (Psalm 121), of *remembering* the good things God has done

(Psalm 143), and of *singing* and *praising* God for his constancy and goodness (Psalms 149, 150). Perhaps it is the very last line of the psalter that sums up the quality of prayer as understood by God's people, Israel . . . "let everything that breathes praise Yahweh! Alleluia." (Psalm 150:6). If we examine the experience of prayer as shared by our Jewish forebears in the faith, we learn that prayer ,is as essential to human life as *breathing*.

Many of us, however, are capable of going through our entire day, or even longer, without praying. Obviously we could not similarly refrain from breathing! How can we account for the seeming gap that exists between our experience and that of our ancestors in the faith?

Harvey Cox, author of *The Secular City* (1965) and a perceptive analyst of the effects of cultural and political currents upon religion, cites the desacralization which exists in modern society. The technological and scientific evolution of humanity seems to have created an atmosphere of individualism and self-sufficiency which affords little support for the activity of praying. This does not mean that Christians are praying less today than in other eras, but it does underscore the struggle which has become integral to the Christian experience of praying. In one of his thought-provoking poems, T.S. Eliot (1888-1965) described the situation of contemporary society in this way: "In other ages, people left God for other gods, but today, they have left God for no god at all." While this a-religious atmosphere plagues modern humanity, and threatens the "spiritual breathing" which is prayer, this was not the atmosphere in which both the Hebrew and Christian Scriptures were recorded.

In their very essence, the Jewish, and later the Christian communities of believers, were communities of prayer. Of course, as any careful reader of history may argue, the Greeks also prayed to their gods, as did the Egyptians, Babylonians, Sumerians, Assyrians, etc. However, there is a critical difference between the prayer of a people for whom the divine is an undifferentiated presence or force in the world, and in the praying of a people to whom the divine has been revealed in a personal way in human history.

For both Jews and Christians, prayer is more than an acknowledgment of a force or power greater than humanity which must be appeased or placated. Rather, praying is an active, attentive response to the prior initiative of a personal God who has chosen to speak a word into time and space and the human heart. The God of the Judaeo-Christian experience reveals in order to invite, to challenge, to guide, to enlighten, to give. As John Sheets has explained, the revelation of God to humankind has an "imperative quality." Jeremiah chose to describe the power of God's word in more graphic terms, "You have seduced me, Yahweh, and I have let myself be seduced; you have overpowered me. You were the stronger . . . I used to say I will not speak in his name any more. Then there seemed to be a fire burning in my heart . . . I could not restrain it" (Jeremiah 20:7-9). Because of this imperative or compelling quality of God's Word, the human response to that word involves a dynamic process of alert listening, careful consideration and decisive action. Samuel and Isaiah stand out as mod-

> **PRAYER is wHAT HAppENS wHEN THE bELiEVER bECOMES AWARE of THE COMpELLiNG pRESENCE of God.**

els of prayer in the Hebrew Scriptures. After his prayerful experience of Yahweh, Samuel's thoughtful response was: "Speak, Lord, your servant is listening," and he lived to enact the mission he received (1 Samuel 3). Isaiah responded to his experience of God with the commitment: "Here I am, Lord, send me" (Isaiah 6).

Readers of the Scriptures can trace the same dynamic throughout salvation history. To the revelation of God as creator, praying believers respond in grateful wonder as blessed creatures. To the revelation of this word as liberator from Egypt, a praying Israel responded in a song of freedom and joy. To the revelation of God's Word of guidance for humanity in the law, Israel struggled to respond, though not always successfully, in a prayer of faithful living.

In studying and meditating upon the Jewish heritage of the faith, it becomes clear that prayer is what happens when the believer becomes aware of the compelling presence of God. In other words, prayer is what we do, as well as who we are, and who we become in response to the God who is constantly in the process of self-revelation to humanity.

Reflections

1. What is your personal definition of prayer?
2. Has that definition changed over the course of your life?
3. Comment on the following statement: "Prayer is as essential to human life as breathing."

Chapter Two

A Never-Ending Dialogue

Shema Yisroel, Adonoi Elohenu Adonoi Echod!

"Hear, O Israel, the Lord is our God, the Lord is One!" (Deuteronomy 6:4)

For over 2,500 years, these words have summoned the believing Jewish community to prayer. Three times during the day, our Jewish ancestors in the faith answered this call and responded to God with a prayer that consecrated their morning (9:00 a.m.), noon, and afternoon (3:00 p.m.) activities to God. Some Jewish historians trace the morning prayer to Abraham (Genesis 19:27), the noon prayer to Isaac (Genesis 26:25) and the afternoon prayer to Jacob (Genesis 28:11). These patriarchs of the Jewish faith were ever alert to the presence of God, and their eagerness to respond to that presence has provided their descendants with a rich heritage of prayer.

Perhaps the most outstanding characteristic of Jewish biblical prayer is the *confidence* with which people approached God. Encouraged by the psalmist who reminded his contemporaries, "The Lord is near to those who call" (Psalm 145:18), the rabbis believed that even "if all the world should pray at once, God will hear the prayers of each one." Confidence in prayer does not mean *self-* confidence. On the contrary, the source of the believer's confidence lies outside him/herself and is found in God. God's power and holiness, God's goodness and constant

40

love inspire unswerving trust and an almost daring confidence. Recall the prayer of Abraham who bartered with God over the city of Sodom. Completely confident in God's fidelity, even to sinful people, Abraham was not afraid to "draw near" to God in prayer and to "speak up again and again." As the Genesis author tells us, Abraham "persisted" in his interchange with God, and his prayer was realized (Genesis 18:20-32).

Job exhibited a similar confidence in the goodness of God. Recall the odyssey of the man from Uz. Described as "an upright and blameless man who feared God and avoided evil," Job systematically suffered the loss of everything and everyone in his life. When family and friends advised him to "curse God and die" (Job 2:9), Job was unrelenting in his confidence. Although his prayer ran the gamut of human emotions, from anger and frustration to sorrow and self-loathing, Job never lost his faith. He dared to challenge and to call God to task for what he perceived as an injustice, but he never dared to refrain from praying. In the end, Job expressed his confident prayer in this way, "I know that my redeemer lives . . . I know that you can do all things, Lord, and that no purpose of yours can be hindered!" (Job 19:25, 42:2).

Like Abraham and like Job, the prayer of Israel was marked by confi-

> EVEN WHEN bELiEVERS GROW lAX ANd/OR SiLENT iN PRAYER, God NEVER CEASES TO COMMUNiCATE; THE dialOGUE WHicH is PRAYER NEVER ENds.

dence. Israel had come to know and experience God through the covenant relationship; having called Israel to intimacy, God remained ever faithful. Despite a long history, checkered by numerous instances of idolatry, immorality, laxness and inauthentic worship, Yahweh had remained a constant companion and protector. Israel had centuries of experiences upon which to base its confident prayer. Even when Israel grew silent in its prayer, God never ceased to communicate; generation after generation of prophets spoke God's word in an effort to keep alive the dialogue which is prayer.

> When God spoke the word who is Jesus into time and space, the dialogue of prayer between God and humankind became personal and intimate in a way that it had never been before.

But at a certain point in human history, the tone of that dialogue changed radically. God spoke an ultimate and absolute Word to humanity in the person and mission of Jesus. Perhaps the first-century B.C.E. author of Wisdom had *anticipated* this unique moment in history when he proclaimed, "When peaceful silence lay over all, and night had run half of her swift course, down from the heavens, from a royal throne, leapt your all-powerful Word!" (Wisdom 18:14-15). However, it was the late first-century C.E. authors of the Johannine literature who were privileged to *affirm* the reality with these words: "In the beginning was the Word and the Word was with God and the Word was God. The Word was made flesh and lived among us . . . something which existed since the beginning, that we have heard, and we have seen with our eyes; that we have watched and touched with our hands: the Word who is life!" (John 1:1,14; 1 John 1:1). When God spoke the Word, who is Jesus, into time and space, and when that Word became enfleshed in human history, the dialogue of prayer between God and humankind became personal and intimate in a way that it had never been before.

This is the essential difference between the Jewish experience of prayer and that of the Christian. As John Sheets has noted, there is both a unity and a radical discontinuity between the two experiences. The *unity* comes from the fact that it is the one and same God who is the Emmanuel – God with us; it is the one and the same God who draws humankind into a covenant relationship. The *discontinuity* comes from the unique event of the Incarnation. The incarnation of the revelation of God is the full flower of all that was promised in the Hebrew scriptures, and "yet its completeness also marks a full giving which is radical in its discontinuity with whatever gift preceded it" (John Sheets). In Jesus, the very essence of God is enfleshed, and this wondrous event draws believers into a new and different mode of prayer. Christian praying is distinct from every other in that it is the listening and sharing, the back and forth, and the give and take of persons who know themselves to be intimately related to one another. Christian praying is the familiar, confident dialogue of the sons and daughters of a good Parent, whose love has become visibly, palpably incarnate in Jesus Christ.

Reflections

1. When you pray, are you as confident as Abraham? as bold as Jeremiah? as blunt as Job?

2. Do you consider the experience of praying as a monologue or a dialogue?

3. How do you address God when you pray? How do you name God?

Chapter Three

A Sacred Place

. . . and the Word became flesh and made his dwelling among us, and we saw his glory, the glory as of the Father's only Son, full of grace and truth. (John 1:14)

In the incarnation, i.e., in the enfleshment of the word in time and space, God said something *new* to the world; in Jesus' words and works God revealed something different concerning the salvation of humankind. Consequently, Christian prayer, which is a response to the prior initiative of God, must also be *new* and different. For one thing, the *place* for meeting God and for engaging in the dialogue which is prayer would be new and distinctive.

Believers of all faiths have traditionally set aside certain places for calling upon their gods. Special care is given to maintain the sacred character of these sites, and pilgrimages are sometimes held to foster faith and zeal among the devotees.

Among the ancient Hebrews, places of special revelation from God were marked by stones and/or altars; some of Abraham's prayerful encounters with God were memorialized at Shechem, Bethel, Mamre and Beersheba (Genesis 12:6,8; 13:18; 21:33). Subsequent generations of believers reverenced these special places as shrines and frequented them in prayer.

When the divine presence and saving plan was revealed to Moses, the ensuing prayerful dialogue imparted a sacred character to Sinai. As Moses and the liberated slaves journeyed from Egypt, through the desert, en route to the Promised Land, the sacred site for encountering God in prayer took on a mobile quality. The portable sanctuary or tent of meeting (also called the tabernacle) became the place for communing with God, because it was there that the *shekinah* or cloud which signified God's presence came to rest; it was there that the glory of the Lord was revealed (Exodus 40:34-38).

After the infiltration and settlement of Canaan and during the period of the monarchy, the temple became the permanent holy place in Israel. Built by Solomon in Jerusalem, the temple was believed to house the presence and glory of the Lord; it was there that Israel came to pray, to offer sacrifice and to renew its covenant relationship with Yahweh (1 Kings 8:10-12).

> In Jesus, humankind received the news that the place for meeting God had become a person.

But with the incarnation of God's Word in Jesus, God revealed something novel to humankind: the *place* for meeting God had become a *person*. The site for experiencing God's glory was now a flesh and blood reality. In Jesus, the Almighty Yahweh has come to dwell, or more literally, "to pitch a tent among us." Both Luke and John make this point very clearly in their respective gospels.

In his infancy narrative, the Lucan evangelist portrayed Jesus at a young age being found in the temple, claiming to be about the business of God (Luke 2:41-52). That "business," as it were, was the very presence of God in the temple. From then on, it would be the "business" of Jesus to be a source of that presence for others . . . to incarnate in his person and in his mission the presence of God for all whom he would meet. Because of this, Jesus would later explain: "No one knows God except the Son and anyone to whom the Son wishes to reveal God" (Luke 10:22), and "Who sees me sees God" (John 14:9), and "I am in the Father and the Father is in me" (John 14:10). Jesus would also encourage his disciples to pray in the "*new* temple" of his presence: "Where two or three are gathered together in my name, there I am in the midst of them" (Matthew 18:20).

All four evangelists relate the episode of Jesus' cleansing of the temple. Turning out the money-changers and animal-sellers, Jesus declared, "My home should be a house of prayer . . . " (Isaiah 56:7, Mark 11:17, Matthew 21:13, Luke 19:46). The Johannine narrative includes Jesus' prediction of the destruction of the temple: "Destroy this temple and in three days I will raise it up," and then notes that Jesus was "speaking about the temple of his body" (John 2:19,21). In both prophetic word and action, Jesus made it clear that: (1) the sanctuary of the temple as a place of prayer and of meeting God was being replaced by himself, and (2) that the system of sacrifice in the temple as a way of prayer and of meeting God would be obviated by the sacrifice of his own body on the cross.

With the temple of his body destroyed and risen, and with his once-and-for-all sacrifice making unnecessary and meaningless all other sacrifices, how and where would Jesus' future disciples meet and pray to God? In the decades following his resurrection, and empowered and enlightened by the Holy Spirit, the followers of Jesus became gradually aware that they *themselves*, as the *Body of Christ*, constituted the *new temple*. In his letters, Paul helped the emerging church to understand itself in this light. Just as *each* believer is a holy place or temple of God insofar as he/she is a member of the Body of Christ (1 Corinthians 6:15, 12:27) and a dwelling place of the Holy Spirit (1 Corinthians 6:19, Romans 8:11), so is the Church the temple of God, founded on the cornerstone of Jesus Christ (1 Corinthians 3:10-17, 2 Corinthians 6:16-18).

> Through the power of the Holy Spirit, the believing community, in each and in all of its members, becomes a sacred place where God's presence can be experienced.

As such, the believing community, in each and in all of its members, continues to be a sacred place where God's presence is made manifest to the world and wherein the world can meet God in the dialogue and holy union of prayer. When the privilege and responsibility of *being a holy place* boggles the mind and threatens to weaken even the firmest resolve, believers can find courage in the promise of Jesus: "Those who love me will keep my word and my Father will love them and we will come to them and make our home in them" (John 14:23).

Great God, we open our hearts and hands, our minds and spirits to be a silent and listening welcome for your Word. Come, Creator, Savior, Spirit, make your home in me so that I may know You and thereby become a place where others can meet you and come home to you. AMEN.

Reflections

1. Where is your favorite place to pray?
2. Do you ever think of yourself as a holy place?

CHAPTER FOUR

INCARNATIONAL PRAYER

. . . he has become man to make it possible for us to love as he has loved us. He makes himself the hungry one, the naked one, the homeless one, the sick one, the one in prison, the lonely one, the unwanted one, and he says: "You did it to me." (Mother Teresa of Calcutta)

With these words a holy woman revealed her noble heart, her deep faith, and her profound understanding of the mystery of the incarnation. Having established that God has said something *new* to humanity in Jesus, the human response to God which is prayer should also become *new*, perhaps some consideration of the quality of prayer is warranted. If prayer is truly to be authentic, then, like the one who prompts prayer within the human heart, it must be incarnational. It is the incarnational quality of Christian prayer which impels the believer to translate his/her response to God in prayer into his/her daily life and to enflesh that response in service, care, compassion and love for others. It is the incarnational quality of prayer which is so well-exemplified in Mother Teresa of Calcutta.

> **AUTHENTIC PRAYER MUST ALSO BE INCARNATIONAL.**

Born Agnes Gonxha Bojaxhiu in 1910 in Skopje, Macedonia,

Mother Teresa first joined the Irish Loreto Sisters and became a missionary in India. After nine years of working as a geography teacher within the community, Mother Teresa understood that she was being called to realize her love for God by tending to the needs of the *poorest* members of the Body of Christ. Through her daily dialogue with God in prayer, Mother Teresa realized the challenge of incarnating the presence of Christ in the world and seeking out that incarnate presence in the faces and bodies of the sick, the homeless and dying poor. Taking Matthew 25:31-46 as her inspiration, Mother Teresa has enabled the rest of us to look into her wrinkled, beautiful and transparent face and to see there the face of Christ; she has invited us to enter into the prayer which is her life and thereby to meet God.

Like Jesus, Mother Teresa understood that no one stands alone before God. We do not pray as a child of God but as *children* of the one Abba, God and as brothers and sisters of Jesus. Therefore, our prayer and the effective expression of our prayer in our daily life should take into account those others with whom we form the Body of Christ.

Jesus' teaching, as preserved in Matthew's gospel, makes this incarnational and social dimension of prayer a priority for believers. "So then, if you are bringing your offering to the altar, and there remember that your brother or sister has something against you, leave your offering there before the altar, go and be reconciled with them first and then come back and present your offering" (Matthew 5:23-24). There can be no true communion in prayer with God if there is no true communion with one another. The author of the Johannine letters has gone even further in his claiming that believers who are alienated from one another thereby threaten their very relationship with God:

> *Anyone who says "I love God" and hates his brother or sister is a liar, since a person who does not love the neighbor that he can see cannot love God whom he has never seen. So this is the commandment that God has given us: if we love God, we should love our sisters and brothers.* (1 John 4:20-21)

In order to aspire to this incarnational quality in prayer, the believer's daily existence must be characterized by wholeness and not by a series of dichotomies. *The Pastoral Constitution on the Church in the Modern World* has acknowledged that "the split between the faith which many profess and their daily lives serves to be counted among the more serious errors of our age" (#43). Due to the exigencies of modern living, we experience tension and a sense that we conduct our life in two different worlds. We perceive as *sacred* that which allows us an experience of God, and as *secular* that which keeps us from God. There is a tendency to dichotomize body and soul, temporal and eternal. What happens when these dichotomies harden, says Kevin Irwin, is that we absent ourselves from the temporal, physical and secular, and try to live life in an escape mode. "Save my soul" becomes the goal and motto of this view of reality.

What is missing in this perception is an integrated approach to life which understands that the secular and the sacred, body and soul, temporal and eternal are to be held together and balanced through the activity of Christian prayer. Prayer empowers the believer to integrate the many and diverse aspects of human existence and to find a stable center in Christ. From that center we can view all things, our world and one another, with a clarity of vision which was exemplified in the person and mission of Jesus.

The great spiritual author and Trappist monk, Thomas Merton, once wrote:

> *A Christianity that despises the world is not truly worthy of the name . . . There is no genuine holiness without this dimension of human and social concern. Finding God (in prayer) means more than abandoning all things that are not God, and emptying oneself of images and desires . . . To find God, one must find oneself. But one cannot do that in isolation from the rest of mankind (sic). We must give ourselves to others. For it is precisely in the recovery of our union with our brothers (sic) in Christ that we discover God and know him (sic) . . . and we experience his (sic) mercy and are liberated from the prison of our self-concern.*

Louis Evely advised believers to be honest in prayer and not to let "prayer be our alibi." In other words, if we tell someone, "I'll pray for you," we are not excused from also doing something to incarnate that prayer. For example, in our graces before meals we pray, "Bless us, O Lord, and these your gifts . . . "; sometimes we add, " . . . and bless those who have prepared our food." Or perhaps we even say, " . . . and give bread to those who have none," after which we settle down to a hearty meal and let God take care of the rest of humankind. That kind of prayer is an alibi. Authentic prayer would include, "Enable us to provide bread for those who have none." Sincere

> FOR TRUE disciplEs of JESUS, pRAYER CANNOT bE AN alibi.

prayer compels us to make bread and to be bread for the hungry. This is the prayer we see exemplified in Mother Teresa; it is to this quality of prayer that each of us is called.

Reflections

1. What are the mutual responsibilities of those who unite their voices and pray . . . *Our* Father, *Our* Mother, *Our* God?

2. What does it mean to *be* bread for others?

CHAPTER FIVE

THE LORD'S PRAYER (PART I)

He was praying in a certain place
and when he had finished,
one of his disciples said to him,
"Lord, teach us to pray." (Luke 11:1)

When Jesus' disciples approached him with the request, "teach us to pray," they did not come to him from a background which was ignorant of prayer. Theirs was a spiritual heritage enriched by the prayers of almost two millennia of believers. From the time of Abraham, who prayed to God as *El Shaddai* (God of the mountain), faithful Jews welcomed the presence of God in prayer. Each successive generation praised God's glory, thanked God for God's goodness, begged forgiveness and confidently presented their needs. Jesus' contemporaries prayed in the Jerusalem temple, in their village synagogues and in the familial warmth of their homes. As beneficiaries of this rich tradition, Jesus' disciples knew *how* to pray. Their request of Jesus expressed a desire to pray *as he did*, but they were asking for more than a lesson or a set of fixed words. The disciples were asking to enter into the very relationship which Jesus shared with his Abba, God. They were asking to share in Jesus' basic orientation in life. They desired to experience the divine presence and to look at God as Jesus. In response to the request of his disciples, Jesus revealed to them (and to us) the very principle by which he lived and for which he gave his life.

THE LORD'S PRAYER CAN ANd should guide ANd inspire All OUR COMMUNICATION with God.

The fact that the *Lord's Prayer* has been preserved in two *distinct* versions (Matthew 6:9-15 and Luke 11:2-4) with *different* wording, and *different* numbers of petitions, should alert as to the fact that Jesus did not intend to hand on to us a *fixed* formula of words to be repeated verbatim. Rather, Jesus has shared with us a *pattern* or a *model* for prayer. Therefore the Lord's Prayer is not only a prayer which we are privileged to repeat in itself, but it is a prayer which will inspire all our other communications with God.

The first element of this simple but comprehensive pattern is the fact that believers may call upon God as *Abba*, God. To pray the prayer Jesus gave is to acknowledge and to renew our relationship as son or daughter of a loving Parent rather than as self-sufficient designers and guides of our own destiny. To accept and to call upon God as Parent is to let go of all our other idolatrous and vain conceptions of God. Voltaire, an 18th-century French philosopher once said, "God made man to his image and likeness and man has returned the compliment!" In the Lord's Prayer, Jesus challenges his disciples to look at God, not as the figment of their wishfulness or imagining, but as God truly and essentially is, as Creator, Provider and Parent.

"To be a parent is an initiative of love; it is to give of oneself without measure. It is to love someone *before* he loves you, when he *does not* love you, and even when he does *not yet exist*" (L. Evely). The power of God's love calls us into being, and sustains and assures our life. Jesus invites us to call upon the great God in heaven as *Abba*, which is the intimate and diminutive name by a child for a parent.

> **The Lord's Prayer helps believers to remain centered on God as the basis of their security.**

In the Matthean version of Jesus' prayer, the qualifier "*Our*" is associated with Abba-God, and the words *our*, *we* and *us* appear no less than nine times in the prayer. The scope of the prayer of Jesus is communal; all whom Jesus invites to call upon God in prayer are drawn together in a solidarity created by and dependent upon the parental love of God. In this special prayer, we meet not only God, but one another and every other child of God. We who dare to call God *Father* or *Mother* must also dare to look at one another and recognize the faces of sisters and brothers.

The second element in the pattern of Jesus' prayer is a challenge to center one's life, energies, and system of values on God. When we pray, "*your* kingdom come, *your* will be done," we make God the basis of our security, and the motivation for all our actions. To acquiesce to the divine will is to welcome into our lives the love and wisdom of God, who loved the world and gifted it with Jesus so that we might have eternal life (John 3:16).

Those who accept the daily challenge of centering themselves on God will gain new strength and insight in balancing all the other aspects of human existence, viz., career, relationships, social pursuits, political choices, economic struggles, etc. Values will be more readily clarified, perspective more easily acquired and trials more realistically endured. "Your will be done" is not a sigh of resignation at something that cannot be changed, but an affirmation of infinite possibilities and blessings.

The third element in the pattern of prayer taught by Jesus is a request for God's constant care, " . . . give us this day our daily bread." This request hinges on the term *daily*, or *epiousios* in Greek. Because this is the sole occurrence of this word in all of the New Testament, its precise meaning has been difficult to ascertain. A compound word, *epiousios* could pertain to *being* or to *coming*. If it has to do with *being*, then the prayerful request is for bread which supports physical existence as well as bread which is necessary to spiritual thriving. Commentators throughout the centuries (Jerome, Augustine) have identified this "bread for *being,*" as all that is needed for physical sustenance as well as the sacramental nourishment of the Eucharist.

Because of its uniqueness, Origen suggested that perhaps the evangelists *invented* the term *epiousios*. But archeologists have recently unearthed an ancient shopping list wherein *epiousios* referred to the supplies which would be needed for the coming day. If the word *epiousios* has to do with *coming*, then the prayer would be for bread for the coming day, and stresses the necessity of living one day at a time, leaving the uncertain future in God's hands.

In either case, Jesus' prayer invites believers to open their hands with trusting expectation to accept all they need from God; as the one who has fulfilled *past* needs, and oversees *present* needs, God also assures believers that their *future* needs will be generously anticipated and answered.

Reflections

1. What is the daily bread for which you pray?
2. What are the implications of the term *Our* in the Our Father or Lord's Prayer?

Chapter Six

The Lord's Prayer (Part II)

In addition to being an expression of trust and confidence in God, the Lord's prayer is also a confession of the human need for divine forgiveness and protection. Prayed by believers for centuries, the Lord's Prayer has inspired sinners to conversion and ordinary people to extraordinary holiness. One such individual was Ignatius of Antioch.

As he traveled to Rome to be martyred, in chains and escorted by soldiers, the early second-century saint wrote several letters in which he witnessed to his deep faith in God. Among Ignatius' letters was a statement which is a commentary on the quality of his prayer life: "I hear within myself something like a sound of running water, which says, 'Come to the Father'" (Epistle to the Romans #7). Ignatius had come to know the presence of God in prayer and had the joy of experiencing that presence as a compelling call to union.

> **Prayer empowers the believer to face the "beast" of sin and to overcome the "beast" with forgiveness.**

When Jesus taught his disciples to pray as he did, he shared with them his basic orientation in life, viz., a daily and growing union with God, who was the source and center as well as the goal of Jesus' existence. Like Jesus, Ignatius drew his strength from God and valued all else in his life according to that relationship. To that end, he bravely faced death in Rome and bore the ultimate witness to the one whom he had come to know in prayer as Abba-God.

Most of us will not be challenged to the extent that Ignatius was; few of us will be literally torn apart by wild beasts as he was for the sake of his relationship with God. Nevertheless, each of us is challenged to face the "beasts" of sin and alienation which threaten our relationships with God and with one another, and to overcome these "beasts" with forgiveness.

"Forgive us our sins for we forgive everyone in debt to us . . . " (Luke 11:4). Admission of sin and its effects upon our life is a key element of the prayer pattern taught by Jesus. In Aramaic, the language spoken by Jesus and his disciples, the most common word for sin was *choba'*. Scholars believe that William Tyndale (1494-1536), the English Reformer and Bible translator, was the first to use the term *trespass*, and that he did so on the basis of Matthew 6:14-15, which is an amplification of the Lord's Prayer. Centuries before Tyndale, Augustine, bishop of Hippo, also expressed a dislike for the term *debt* because he thought some could conveniently interpret Jesus' prayer as an excuse to avoid payment of their monetary obligations. Nevertheless, *debt* is the intended meaning and the reason for which we are to pray for forgiveness.

In his commentary on the Lord's Prayer, Origen explained, "While a man is alive, there is not a single hour, day or night when he is not a debtor." As human beings lovingly created and enlivened by the very breath of God, we are in debt to God for our very lives. Each day we live

> # BefoRe God, eACH of us is AN indENTURed SERVANT.

we are sustained by God's care, protected by God's strength and nourished by God's gifts of grace. We are, as it were, "indentured" persons.

Recall the practice which existed in this country during colonial times. Would-be settlers from Europe who could not otherwise afford to travel, and/or to reestablish themselves in the New World, entered into contracts of indenture. In some instances, when the terms were settled, the contract was artfully cut into two pieces, with both pieces fitting together like two pieces of a jig-saw puzzle. When the terms of the contract were met and the length of indentured service had expired, the indentured person was given both pieces of the contract as a sign of his/her freedom.

As human beings, we are indentured to God in the sense that we are made in the divine image and likeness, and bound ("contracted") by virtue of that privilege to be faithful to that image. When we are not, we have fallen short of the debt owed to God; we are in need of forgiveness. When we are faithful, then the life that we live is an authentic reflection of the One in whose image we are made. Jesus has come among us to teach us how to "fit together" with our Abba, God, as two pieces of one whole. He has come to show us what it means to live according to God's image. If we love as God loves and forgives, then we become whole and holy, "perfect as God is perfect."

Besides the debt each of us owes to God, we are indebted to one another as social beings; we owe one another support and complementarity, mutual respect and shared strength. Through the example of his life and through his teaching, Jesus extended our social indebtedness to include enemies, those who hate us, those who ask for our coats as well as our shirts, those who press us into service, those who ask us for gifts, and those who wish to borrow from us (Matthew 5:39-48). Those who think that these teachings of Jesus are not to be taken seriously or that these are ideals too lofty to attain, cannot pray the Lord's prayer truthfully. Authentic, sincere prayer is contingent upon a daily acceptance of the challenge of the gospel.

The final aspect of the prayer Jesus taught his disciples concerns temptation, trial and evil. In Greek (the language in which the gospels have been handed on to us) the word *peirasmos* is translated as *both* temptation and trial. No English word does complete justice to the concept of *peirasmos*, which means an *event* or situation which engages a person in a process of decision-making and choosing. Included in this process is the certainty of struggle and the possibility of failure. The person who prays "lead us not into temptation but deliver us from evil" makes certain admissions: The first of these is the peril of the human situation and the allure of sin which affects each of us. Second, this petition confesses the inadequacy of human resources to cope with the situation. In praying the Lord's Prayer, the believer places before God both the peril of the human situation as well as his/her inadequacies, and in utter confidence trusts in the power of God to hear, to give, to deliver and to save.

Among the earliest generations of believers, the Lord's prayer was considered a sign of Christian identity. Catechumens were taught Jesus' prayer shortly before or immediately after their Baptism. As early as 350 C.E., the Lord's Prayer was incorporated into the Mass of the

Faithful, and was so revered that both the eastern and western liturgies introduced the prayer with the phrase, "we dare to say . . . "

While the doxology, "For yours is the kingdom, the power and the glory, forever and ever, Amen," does not appear in any early manuscript of the gospels, it can be traced to the *Didache,* or the Teaching of the Twelve Apostles, an informative Christian document, dated ca. 100 C.E. This same document also recommended that Christians pray the Lord's Prayer three times each day.

Each time we dare to pray this prayer, we enter once again into that special place where God is Abba, where we are loved and cherished children. Each time we pray the Our Father, we center ourselves on God and open ourselves to the divine gifts of bread and forgiveness. Each time we call upon God, we renew our commitment to one another as forgiven and forgiving brothers and sisters. And in those instances when we do not or dare not pray as we ought, St. Paul reminds us that the Holy Spirit comes to aid us in our weakness and to intercede for us with inexpressible groanings . . . empowering us to cry out "Abba, God!" (Romans 8:15,26)

Reflections

1. What is the debt we owe to God?
2. How are we indebted to one another?

The Parables of Jesus

CHAPTER ONE

Why Did Jesus Teach in Parables?

Who is there among us who doesn't love a story? Whenever a speaker or a parent or a teacher intones the familiar phrase, "Once upon a time," everyone of us, from three to 93, settles down and prepares to be amused, entertained and shuttled on a delightful flight of fancy.

> **Parables are earthly stories with a heavenly meaning.**

Stories bring relief to our routine and sometimes humdrum lives; stories punctuate with laughter and sometimes, even with tears, the seemingly banal flow of our existence. It is not surprising, then, that Jesus told stories, that he employed a story mode and style for grasping the attention of his hearers. But unlike the fairy tales parents read to send their little ones off to sleep, Jesus' stories were intended to *alert* his hearers, to rouse their private and public consciousness to a new way of thinking, to a new way of being, to a new way of perceiving salvation and the demands of his truth upon humanity. The vehicle Jesus used to tell his stories is called a *parable*.

Not unique to or original with Jesus, the parable was a popular literary genre in the ancient world. Politicians, philosophers, orators and rabbis all made use of this particular vehicle of communication. Very simply, a parable

may be defined as an earthly story with a heavenly significance. The basic function of a parable is comparison, i.e.,
a parable places something familiar alongside something
less familiar in order to illumine the latter. The English
word *parable* comes from the Greek, *parabole*, which
means "the placing of things side by side." The Hebrew
word for parable is *mashal*, a word which represented
many verbal images, e.g., similes, metaphors, proverbs,
riddles, etc.

Parables should not be confused with fables and/or
allegories. *Fables* are built upon fantasy, and the principal
characters in fables are usually animals endowed with hu-
man-like capacities and feelings. *Parables*, however, are
true-to-life, regardless of whether the framework of the
story is or is not historical. *Allegories* are prolonged
metaphors, stories in which every detail, every character
and event has a parallel and/or symbolic meaning. In contrast to the allegory, the parable usually supports a single
idea and conveys one simple meaning. As G.H. Hubbard
has observed, the parable is like a lens "which gathers
many of the sun's rays and brings them to focus upon a
single point." Modern readers should remember that the
details of a particular parable have little significance in
themselves. Rather, they simply serve as a vehicle for the
point or basic message of the parable.

Why are these distinctions important? Readers of the
early Church Fathers will recall there was a time when the
parables Jesus told were treated as allegories. As C.H.
Dodd has noted, the results were fantastically interesting,
but often obscured the point Jesus wished to communicate. For example, Augustine, in his interpretation of the
Good Samaritan parable (Luke 10:30-37), taught that: the
traveler was a symbol for Adam; Jerusalem was the city
of peace from which Adam fell; Jericho represented hu-

man mortality; the thieves were the devil and his angels who robbed Adam of immortality; the priest and Levite represented the corrupt Old Testament liturgy; the Samaritan was Christ; the inn was the Church, and the innkeeper was Paul. As Dodd pointed out, these identifications would have amazed Jesus. Indeed, Jesus' original message and the point of the parable, viz., the challenge to love all others as neighbors and without limit, has been totally obscured by allegorical embellishment.

Why did Jesus teach in parables? A puzzling passage in Mark's gospel suggests that Jesus spoke in parables in order to confuse and to conceal rather than to clarify and reveal. Speaking to his disciples, Jesus said, "To you has been given the secret of the kingdom of God, but for those outside, everything is in parables; so that they may indeed see but not perceive, and may indeed hear but not understand; lest they should turn again and be forgiven" (Mark 4:11-12). Based on a similar text from Isaiah (6:9-10), this passage should be understood not as a *reason for* parabolic teaching but as a *reflection on* what transpired as a *result* of the parables of Jesus. To suggest that Jesus spoke in parables in order to create misunderstanding falsifies the intentions both of the gospel tradition and of Jesus. But this interpretation does contain a certain element of truth; for the hearer who resists Jesus' teaching, the parables are *indeed* a puzzle.

> EACH TIME A PARABLE IS READ, BELIEVERS ARE CONFRONTED WITH A CHALLENGE.

Another passage from the gospels more accurately describes the purpose of Jesus' parables: "Do not suppose that my mission on earth is to spread peace. My mission is to spread not peace but division. I have come to set a man at odds with his father, a daughter with her mother, a daughter-in-law with her mother-in-law; in short, to make a man's enemies those of his own household" (Matthew 10:34-36; Luke 12:49-53). In this harsh statement is the key for unlocking the mystery of the parables. Jesus, by his very presence, created division upon the earth. Foretold in the song of Simeon (Luke 2:35) and described by the author of Hebrews (4:12), Jesus' presence and his teachings were like a sword which pierced to the heart and sharply divided his hearers. He came to bring not calm but crisis: a crisis of decision, a crisis of judgment, a crisis of faith. The parables represent that crisis as they offer to all who read them an ultimatum: Will you stand with Jesus or against him? Those who humbly opened themselves to Jesus' truth and who accepted the challenge of his word understood the parables; those who did not remained in the darkness of their own disbelief.

Contemporary readers of the gospel might better appreciate the parables by approaching each one as an invitation to conversion. Every time a parable is read, there is presented therein a challenge from Jesus to examine oneself with regard to the values put forth in the gospel, to grow in faith and to deepen in one's commitment to the building up of Jesus' body, the Church. Inevitably those who choose to respond to the challenge of the parables will experience a certain share of "division" and of the "sword." These sufferings represent a participation in the cross and are integral to the life of the disciple. But, just as the parables challenge and test, so too do these precious stories nourish and sustain in hope all who put their faith in Jesus.

Reflections

1. What is the difference between an allegory and a parable?

2. How is this difference important for understanding the parable?

Chapter Two

What Do the Parables Teach?

The Reign of God

Before discussing the more significant issues which are brought to our attention by the parables, it is important that contemporary readers of the gospel appreciate the parables for all the *unintended* information they offer. More than any other type of New Testament literature, the parables provide us with a window into the life and times of Jesus. From the parables, we can gain an understanding of Jewish mores, of wedding feasts, banquet etiquette, agricultural and architectural techniques, economic policies and pastoral customs. From the parables, we may gain insight into the sociopolitical situation of 1st-century Judah, of its relations with the Roman occupation, of its attitude toward foreigners, apostates, etc. While this background material is quite interesting and help-

> **The parables provide their readers with a window into the life and times of Jesus and with a challenge as regards their own life and times.**

ful, its primary function was to serve as a vehicle for a more important message. Couched within the simple events and circumstances of everyday Palestinian life, Jesus taught in parables in order to convey to his contemporaries and to us the truth *about the reign of God.* This was the basic point which Jesus wished to communicate; he did so tirelessly, with a variety of images to a variety of audiences.

Every student of the parables must be aware of the modifications and adaptations which the parables of Jesus have undergone. At times these modifications overshadow the parable's essential message; more often than not, however, the modifications enhance and expand that message. In the past two centuries, scholarly researchers of the scriptures have discovered that Jesus' parables had two historical settings: the first or original setting was that of Jesus' earthly ministry; the other, a later setting, was provided by the early Christian community. A third setting, a literary one, was provided by the scriptural author, i.e., the evangelist and/or an editor, etc.

As Jesus traveled around his native Judea, into Galilee and the region of the Decapolis, he told his stories to the people he met. An excellent teacher, he shaped his parables according to the circumstances of his particular audience. With those who made a living fishing in the Sea of Galilee, Jesus employed a maritime metaphor; with shepherds, a pastoral motif, etc.

No one followed Jesus with a tape recorder or camcorder; no one even took notes of his teachings. After Jesus' death and resurrection, those who believed in him and remembered his teachings circulated their recollections orally. Gradually, the early Church made a collection of the parables they remembered, arranged them according to subject matter and, as C.M. Connick has put it, "pressed them into service. The parables underwent considerable modification when they were employed by the church in its preaching and teaching mission."

Moreover, the translation from Jesus' native Aramaic into Greek also resulted in several alterations of vocabulary and adaptations of symbols, etc. With the ever-expanding Church, it became necessary to substitute a Hellenistic or Greek setting for the original Palestinian one. Because of these developments, some parables were amalgamated; some were expanded, others were reduced, still others underwent an extensive literary and theological evolution, and thereby accrued different meanings and altered significance. Some may be dismayed at the transformation which the parables underwent, transformations which make it impossible to identify with absolute certainty the actual words of Jesus. Instead of becoming discouraged and/or disappointed by these facts, modern readers should rather be moved to better appreciate the efforts made by the early Church to keep alive the message of Jesus and to maintain its relevance in the midst of their developing and changing world.

Jesus' message was actually quite simple: as C.M. Connick has noted, Jesus communicated a few basic concepts with groups or clusters of similar parables. Studying these various parable groups provides an excellent summary of his teaching with regard to:

> JESUS USED THE PARABLES AS A VEHICLE FOR TEACHING ABOUT THE REIGN OF God.

(1) the imminence of the reign of God,

(2) the membership in the reign of God,

(3) the inevitability of God's reign,

(4) the challenge of membership or discipleship,

(5) the supreme value of the reign of God.

First and foremost, Jesus taught his contemporaries about the *imminence of God's reign*. As a result of its nearness, an atmosphere of urgency prevailed, because with the establishment of the reign of God would come judgment, and with judgment would also come reward and/or retribution. Joachim Jeremias, one of the pioneer researchers of the parables, has called those parables which teach of the nearness of God's reign "crisis parables." Each one issues a warning to those who hear it. For example, the parable of the Fig Tree was told by Jesus in an effort to alert his contemporaries to the reign of God, which had become present in his own person. "Learn the lesson of the budding fig tree (Jesus taught) so that when you see this sign you will know that it is near, at the very gates." Later, when the synoptics put down their recollections of this parable, they gave it an eschatological setting (Mark 13:28-29, Matthew 24:32-33, Luke 21:29-31); they adapted Jesus' original announcement of the reign of God in order to refer it to the climax of the world and Jesus' second coming.

Jesus told many other parables concerning the nearness of God's kingdom, e.g., the Wicked or Unfaithful Servant (Matthew 24:45-51, Luke 12:42-46), the parable of the Talents (Luke 19:12-27, Matthew 25:14-28), the Wise and Foolish Maidens (Matthew 25:1-13), etc. A number of these parables (Speck and Plank: Matthew 7:3-5, Luke 6:41-42; Blind Guides: Matthew 15:14, Luke 6:39; Lamp: Mark 4:21, Luke 8:16, Matthew 5:15) were originally directed by Jesus at the leaders of Israel, who should have been the first to perceive and accept God's reign as revealed in Jesus and to lead the people to a similar recognition and acceptance. The early Church recast these parables and applied them to believers in Jesus, whose faith in him and in his return was growing dim.

With the twin parables of the New Wineskins and New Cloth (Matthew 9:16-17, Mark 2:21-22, Luke 5:36-38), Jesus again proclaimed the nearness of the reign of God as the dawn of a new era, which required a new way of thinking and a radical new ethic. Just as new wine would burst an old wineskin and a patch of new cloth would shrink and ruin a garment made of old cloth, so would those who refused to open themselves to Jesus' good news of salvation forfeit the treasure of the God's reign. All who today read the parables concerning the imminence of God's reign are faced with the same challenge as Jesus' original audience. This challenge places believers in a crisis situation. Do we accept the challenge, answer the crisis and choose Jesus and God's reign or do we allow fear, laziness, apathy or other concerns to dissuade us? The parables speak, Jesus calls; the choice is ours.

Reflections

1. How did the early church press the parables into service?

2. What do the parables about the nearness of God's reign teach us?

Chapter Three

Who Is Who in the Kindom* of God?

Membership in the Kindom

Odds-makers would have had a heyday making predictions about Jesus. Statistically speaking, what were the chances of success for a carpenter's son from Nazareth who had little, if any, formal education, no money to speak of and no claim to fame whatsoever? Moreover, this same person took unnecessary risks by contradicting established tradition, by questioning centuries-old ideologies, and by refusing to curry the favors of the political and religious authorities of his day. To add to his troubles, the man from Nazareth dared to insist that he had a *special* relationship with the Holy One of Israel, whom he called "Daddy," "Papa" (*Abba*). He also had the audacity to invite the pariahs of society, viz., the sinners, the sick, adulterous women and even Gentiles (!) to share in that special relationship. Last, but not least in the long list of strikes against him, Jesus insinuated that those whom the self-righteous regarded as outcasts would enjoy not only an equivalent share in the kindom of God, but that those whom the rich despised may even receive a greater share of glory. Indeed, there were very clear indications in Jesus' parables that the self-righteous rich may not even find

---

*   The *Inclusive New Testament* suggest the gender sensitive, albeit, coined word kindom.

> JESUS' PARABLES TURNED THE TRADITIONAL IDEAS ABOUT HOLINESS AND SALVATION ON THEIR EAR.

a home in God's established reign because they had sought their treasures and spent their energies elsewhere.

Precisely what do the parables of Jesus teach about membership in the kindom? The primary principle concerning membership is one of *inclusivity*. In a society which distinguished between rich and poor, and attributed poverty to sin . . . in a culture which sifted through the masses and determined ritual purity by a series of carefully prescribed external behaviors . . . in an environment which fostered the separation of peoples into economic, social, political and moral categories, Jesus taught that the kindom of God is inclusive of all.

Many of Jesus' parables in this regard were addressed to those who considered themselves to be the respectable and deserving heirs of God's blessings. For example, the beautiful triplet parables of the Lost Sheep (Luke 15:1-7), the Lost Coin (Luke 15:8-10), and the Lost Son (Luke 15:11-31) were told to an audience comprised of tax collectors, sinners, Pharisees and scribes. For the tax collectors and sinners, Jesus' teaching offered hope and made them aware of God's special concern for those who have strayed. For the Pharisees and scribes, these parables provided a much-needed lesson, i.e., God rejoices over the return of the repentant and welcomes them with open arms. Through these parables, Jesus challenged the scribes and Pharisees to rethink their traditional values and to open themselves to another point of view concerning their weaker and disadvantaged brothers and sisters. Similar parables, e.g., the Physician and the Sick (Matthew 9:12, Mark 2:17, Luke 5:31), the Two Sons (Matthew 21:28-31), the Two Debtors (Luke 7:41-43), the Pharisee and the

MEMBERSHip iN THE kiNdom of God is iNclusive of All — SAiNTS AS WEll AS SiNNERS.

Publican (Luke 18:10-14), etc., proffered a similar challenge: Those who would belong to the kindom must adopt a new way of looking at one another and learn to respect one another in a humble and loving manner. To put others first, to value others more than oneself . . . these are the keys which will open the gates of God's kindom.

In the parable of the Laborers in the Vineyard (Matthew 20:1-15), all who consider themselves long-suffering and faithful are taught a powerful lesson about God's criteria for admission to the kindom. Recall the story of the farmer who at various hours during the day hired laborers to work in his fields. At the end of the day, he paid the *same* wage to those who had borne the heat of a 12-hour day as well as to those who had spent only an hour at work. Resentment welled up in the hearts of those who worked all day. They felt they deserved more than those who had come later to the fields. Their resentment underscored their lack of understanding of God's ways. God's mercy, for those who turn to the truth "late" in their lives, is not an injustice to those whose entire lives have been spent in faithful service. Human standards of justice do not apply, nor can human imaginations fathom the depths of God's mercy. Because of that mercy, *all* are welcome in the kindom, even those who repent only in their last, dying breath.

Another valuable lesson concerning membership in the kindom can be learned from the parables of the Weeds and the Wheat (Matthew 13:24-30) and the Dragnet (Matthew 13:47-48). Upon discovering that poisonous weeds had sprung up with the wheat, a householder's servants offered to pull up the weeds. No, said the owner of the field, "lest in gathering the weeds you root up the wheat along with them. Let both grow together until the harvest; at harvest time I will tell the reapers, 'Gather the weeds first and bind them in bundles to be burned, but gather the wheat into my barn'" (Matthew 13:29-30). The parable of the dragnet is similar; all objects are gathered indiscriminately into the net and are separated only after the catch is complete. There are several important points here:

(1) The distinction between wheat and weeds, between valuable and nonvaluable objects is not ours to decide. In other words, membership and/or nonmembership in the kindom is God's sole prerogative;

(2) In the meantime, wheat and weeds will grow alongside one another. Nevertheless, neither should presume to judge the value of the other. That judgment is God's alone.

(3) The definitive distinction between wheat and weeds took place *only* at harvest time. For humanity, God's definitive decision about membership in the kindom will come at the end of time. Until then we are blessed with the gift of time . . . time to change our "weediness" into wheat . . . time to be converted, heart, mind and spirit to Christ.

In conclusion, then, the parables paint for us a wonderful image of the kindom. Membership in that kindom is *God's gift* and is made possible by *God's grace*. There are no dues except the faithful service of a life spent in loving God and discovering the divine will. Those who would belong to God, who would make their hearts a home for God's reign are called to daily growth, frequent repentance and constant thanksgiving for the graciousness and kindness with which God blesses each day. Finally, it should be remembered that those who choose to enjoy the prestige of exclusivity here on earth, i.e., those who pride themselves in moving in society's "best circles," may find themselves "out of place" in God's kindom.

Reflections

1. In the parable of the wheat and weeds, what point offers you the greatest challenge?

2. What part of the parable do you find the most comforting?

"YOUR KINDOM COME". . . THERE IS NO DOUBT ABOUT THE INEVITABILITY OF THE KINGDOM

When Jesus' disciples came to him and requested, "Lord, teach us to pray," Jesus instructed them to pray, "Abba, God, holy is your name, *your kindom come.*" These opening lines in the prayer, which we have all learned to love as the "Lord's Prayer," is more a declaration than a petition. In the statement "your kindom come," Jesus proclaimed, with absolute certainty, the fact that God's reign would be realized. This proclamation of

> TO PRAY, "YOUR KINDOM COME" IS TO AFFIRM THE INEVITABILITY OF GOD'S REIGN.

the sureness or inevitability of the kindom was another of the major concepts which Jesus taught by means of his parables.

In the twin parables concerning the Mustard Seed and the Leaven (Mark 4:30-32, Matthew 13:31-33, Luke 13:18-21), those who yearn for the consummation of the kindom will find encouragement. These short parables assure those who read them that God's reign will inevitably and undoubtedly come. Mustard seeds aren't really the

FROM A SMALL AND INSIGNIFICANT BEGINNING, God HAS BROUGHT ABOUT GREAT AND WONDERFUL RESULTS.

smallest of all seeds; still they are quite minuscule when compared to the ten or twelve-foot shrub which they produce. So too, anyone who has ever baked bread knows that a relatively small amount of leaven or yeast is sufficient to make quite a large mass of dough to rise. No doubt, Jesus' disciples probably felt as small as mustard seeds when they compared their influence and numbers to their Jewish counterparts. They felt as insignificant as a small measure of leaven compared to the great masses of peoples which constituted the empire of Rome. This was precisely the point of Jesus' parable. From even such a small and insignificant thing as a mustard seed, a great shrub can grow. From even such a small and seemingly insignificant group as Jesus' first followers, God was able to bring about great and wonderful results. The striking contrast between the tiny beginning and astounding end-result underscored God's sovereignty and the inevitability of the power of God's reign.

Another parable which attested to the inevitability of the kindom is that of the Seed Growing Secretly (Mark 4:26-29). In this story, Jesus compared God's reign to a harvest. Again, as in the parables of the mustard seed and the leaven, the reader is confronted with a sharp contrast. As Joachim Jeremias has observed: "The inactivity of the farmer after sowing is vividly depicted; his life follows its ordered round of sleeping and waking night and day. Without the farmer's worry or help the seed grows from stalk to ear and from ear to ripened corn, in an unceasing process of growth until the harvest." What could be more amazing? Even though the farmer was unaware of how it happened, the grain was suddenly ripe and ready for the sickle. For Jesus' followers, these parables were a source of strength; from their small and uninfluential group a mighty assembly would surely and eventually emerge, an assembly (in Greek *ekklesia*: church), the members of which would constitute God's ever-growing, ever-emerging kindom. Later, Mark's community adapted these parables to encourage those who had grown despondent about the delay of Jesus' return. As wondrously as the mustard seed grows into a great bush, as readily as the leaven can raise a great mass of dough, and as silently as the seed which grows without the farmer's knowledge, the parables taught that Jesus would surely come again and bring his own home with him to glory.

A final point concerning the certainty of the establishment of God's reign can be found in the parable of the sower (Matthew 13:3-8, Mark 4:3-8, Luke 8:5-8). In order to fully understand Jesus' intended message, it is necessary to set aside, for the moment, the early Church's added interpretation of the parable (Matthew 13:18-23, Mark 4:13-20, Luke 8:11-15) as well as any knowledge we may have of contemporary agricultural techniques. To the modern farmer, the sower's method of planting may seem rather senseless. To throw seed indiscriminately, allowing it to fall on footpaths, among thorns or rocks seems to be an exercise in futility. But, in Palestine, unlike the U.S., sowing *precedes* planting, and in spite of the many difficulties faced by the farmer in this parable (birds, thorns, weather, drought), he expected and he reaped an abundant harvest. Here in the U.S. a return of forty- or fifty-fold would be an excellent wheat harvest, but Jesus spoke of as much as a hundredfold! Obviously, his parable referred to the abundant and overflowing goodness of God.

For those disciples who, like the farmer, worked in the fields of humanity for the sake of the kindom, the parable promised an abundance of fruit for their labors. Despite all adversity and against all odds, the kindom would grow; God's reign would become an undeniable and an inevitable reality. By the time the Sower parable was incorporated into the written gospels, it had undergone an adaptation in interpretation; the Church's interpretation was then incorporated into the parable by the evangelists. According to its later meaning, the parable taught a lesson about the word of God. The seed symbolized God's word, while the different soils, rocks, etc., represented those who either heard and acted upon the word or did not.

At this second level of its development, the parable challenged Christians to remain open to the Word of God, to welcome the Word into their hearts and to bring forth the fruit which the Word inspires. Perhaps the early community understood their receptivity to the Word as their continuing response to the Incarnate Word, Jesus Christ, and as a fulfillment of the prophecy of Isaiah: "For just as from the heavens the rain and snow come down and do not return there till they have watered the earth, making it fertile and fruitful, giving seed to those who sow and bread to those who eat, so shall my Word be that goes forth from my mouth; it shall not return to me void but shall do my will, achieving the end for which I sent it" (Isaiah 55:10-11). Both meanings of the parable, the original message concerning the inevitability of the kindom and the secondary interpretation concerning the importance of responding to the Word, remain as challenges to all who in faith come to the gospels for nourishment and strength.

Reflections

1. What is the original meaning of the parable of the sower?
2. How did the early church adapt and interpret this parable?
3. How would you adapt and apply it to your own life situation?

CHAPTER FIVE

Cost of Discipleship

THE CHALLENGE OF THE PARABLES

Dietrich Bonhöeffer, a German theologian who endured torture and martyrdom during the Nazi regime, once said, "When Jesus calls a man, he bids him 'Come and die!'" From his experiences at Tegel prison and at the death camps at Buchenwald and Flossenburg, Bonhöeffer learned that discipleship costs not less than everything. This great Christian martyr understood one of the most important concepts Jesus taught in his parables, viz., that membership in the kindom or discipleship is a challenge which engages every human thought, energy and desire in an absolute and unending commitment.

IN JESUS' COMPANY, THERE IS NO ROOM FOR MEDIOCRE, HESITANT OR "WEEKEND" disciples.

Jesus was not one to mince words; he made it clear that those who would follow him should do so wholeheartedly. There was no room in his company for mediocre, hesitant or "weekend" disciples. With harsh Semitic idiomatic statements such as, "If anyone comes to me and does not hate their father and mother, spouse and children, brothers and sisters, yes and even their own life, they cannot be my disciple" (Luke 14:26), and "Leave the dead to bury their own dead" (Luke 9:60), and "Once a person has put hand to the plow, that person cannot look back" (Luke 9:62), Jesus taught that only those who made the reign or kindom of God their *top priority* could be his disciples. Having established the priority of the reign of God, these Semitisms beg for further explanation. The negative reference to hating parents, spouses, children, etc., should be understood as a positive challenge to love God *more* and to allow that love to inform and guide all other loves. As heartless as the phrase sounds . . . "leave the dead to bury their dead" . . . it is not without deep sensitivity for the exigencies of human life. Recall the context of the statement: Jesus had invited someone to be a disciple. "Follow me," Jesus called. In reply, the person said, "Let me go first and bury my father." In actual fact, the father had not yet died and probably wasn't even ill. The would-be disciple was indicating that Jesus' call was not convenient and that at a later time, viz., when future familial responsibilities were taken care of, perhaps discipleship would be possible. Jesus' response affirmed the fact that the challenge of discipleship cannot be postponed.

In the saying about the plow, disciples are taught that commitment to Jesus requires complete and constant attention. Those who take to plowing and look back end up

> JESUS INVITES BELIEVERS TO ENTER INTO DISCIPLESHIP, APPRISED THAT IT COSTS NOT LESS THAN EVERYTHING.

with crooked, useless furrows. Those who commit to Jesus and look to their past with regret at what may have been or at all they have left behind will be unauthentic and distracted disciples.

By means of the companion parables of the Tower and the King at War (Luke 14:28-32), Jesus advised his would-be followers to understand and to assess the cost of discipleship for themselves. Recall the Tower parable: A person who wishes to build a tower must first, sit down and calculate the cost of construction. Otherwise, once work has begun and funds run low, the construction will have to be abandoned. This would leave the builder open to mockery: "This person began to build and was not able to finish!"

The case is the same with the king who was plotting against an adversary. What a fool he would be if he did not first sit down with his advisors and plan a strategy to determine whether "he is able with ten thousand to meet him who comes against him with twenty thousand." And if not, while the other is yet a great way off he sends an embassy and asks terms of peace (Luke 14:33). Like the wise tower builder and the warring king, the followers of Jesus are called to enter into discipleship with open eyes and clear heads, apprised of the cost, but willing to meet its demands. Naiveté has no place in the lives of those who accept Jesus' call.

Another challenge Jesus proposed to his would-be disciples was that they embrace a new morality, one which placed love of neighbor on a par with love of God. On one of the many occasions in which Jesus was being questioned with regard to his views on the law, someone asked "which law was the greatest of all?" (Mark 12:28). Jesus replied, "You shall love the Lord your God with all your heart, with all your soul, with all your strength and with all your mind, and your neighbor as yourself" (Mark 12:30-31, Luke 10:27). This in itself was a radical statement. Jesus was, in effect, placing the demands of social justice on a par with devotion and commitment to God. But the Jews who heard Jesus had traditionally understood "neighbor" as a reference only to other Israelites (Leviticus 19:18). To enunciate more clearly his own concept of *neighbor* and the revolutionary morality to which he called his disciples, Jesus told the parable of the Good Samaritan (Luke 10:30-37): A man was accosted and robbed on the seventeen-mile trip from Jerusalem to Jericho. Left for dead, he lay there while a priest and later a Levite passed by. Perhaps they believed him to be dead and feared to become ritually unclean by contact with a corpse? Or perhaps they decided that their predetermined missions were more important than helping the victim of a crime . . . ? Whatever their motives, they chose to pass by without rendering any assistance to the robbed man. Significantly, we are not told of the motivation of the Samaritan either. But his motivation was revealed by his actions. A person despised by the Israelites, the Samaritan behaved in a caring, loving manner; he went out of his way to help. Where the priest and Levite had failed, he had shown himself a loving neighbor. As T. Manson has noted, "The point of the parable is that if a man has love in his heart, it will tell him who his neighbor is. The cost of discipleship is love without limit." This parable challenges those who profess to love Jesus to put aside racial, national and even familial preferences in order to embrace and to serve the needs of all God's people.

The parable of the Sheep and Goats in the judgment scene from Matthew's gospel (Matthew 25:31-46) also underscores the importance and centrality of love. According to the parable, at the end of time the Son of Man will come in glory, and with all the nations assembled before him, he will act as judge. Using the imagery of a shepherd separating sheep from goats, the evangelist went on to explain the criterion upon which the nations would be judged, i.e., the criterion of love, actively expressed in deeds of kindness for the hungry, the thirsty, foreigners, the naked, the sick and the imprisoned. It is in these small and simple deeds that discipleship is learned and that the love of God and neighbor is authentically expressed.

Finally, Jesus challenged his disciples to press their love into service for one another and to be willing to stretch that love to its fullest capacity by freely granting forgiveness to all who ask it. Recall the parable of the Merciless Servant (Matthew 18:23-34). After an audit, the servant's books revealed an enormous and nonrepayable deficit; as punishment, the employer ordered that the servant, his lands, and his family be sold. Throwing himself upon his employer's mercy, the dishonest servant pleaded for time to make renumerations. In his kindness, the employer forgave the entire debt. But the servant learned nothing from his experience. Rather than show a similar forgiveness to a fellow servant who owed him a trifling debt, he callously had him put into prison. In the end the wicked servant was reported to his employer and tortured until his debt was paid.

The point of the parable is quite clear. All who follow Jesus have been forgiven an enormous debt of sin. Forgiven, we must also be forgiving. Loved to the point of Jesus' death on a Cross, we are to love without limit. This is the cost of discipleship, the challenge of the kindom.

Reflection

1. What has been the cost of discipleship in your life?

2. Is the call to love and forgive without limit a practical possibility in today's world?

Chapter Six

"Where Your Treasure Is, There Also Is Your Heart"

The Supreme Value of the Kindom

Imagine yourself in the following situation: Suppose your home were on fire and you had only a minute or two to escape to safety. Aside from your family, what particular thing would you make sure to take with you from the blaze? Obviously, there will be a variety of answers to this question. Some may grab the keys to the car, others their bank records, others may take their insurance policies with them. Still others may run to the closet for a cherished photograph album or a valuable fur coat. A child may choose a pet, a favorite toy or stuffed animal. In these circumstances, what would *you* choose to save and to carry with you? Whatever your answer may be, it may give you a good indication of your value system and priorities in life.

When Jesus moved among the people of Nazareth, Galilee, Judea, etc., he repeatedly challenged

> Those who give all they have for the sake of God's reign have found a wealth which devalues all other currencies.

them to rethink their traditional values, to reevaluate their priorities and to adopt a new way of looking at themselves, at one another, at God and at their world. He urged his hearers to discover those things in life which are truly important and absolutely necessary. The principle or criterion Jesus proposed for properly and truthfully ordering one's values is this: "Seek first the reign of God over you, God's way of holiness, and all things will be given you besides" (Matthew 6:33). Those who seek the kindom of heaven, i.e., those who by faith and through service experience the power of God's reign, will learn the lesson of the gospels, the values which Jesus taught and by which he lived. A pair of short parables from Matthew's gospel graphically illustrate the lesson Jesus wished to teach concerning the supreme value of the kindom. Both parables can be better appreciated if contemporary readers are aware of the historical and cultural situations which spawned them.

The first parable compared God's reign to a Treasure Hidden in a Field (Matthew 13:44). In Jesus' day most people did not entrust their valuables to banks. The Roman occupation, revolts and an unstable economy forced them to do otherwise. Often, people hid their wealth (fine garments, money, jewels) in their homes or somewhere on their property. If these people were killed or died of a sudden illness and had not recovered their wealth or told family members of its location, it may have been left undiscovered in a field for years. This seems to be the background of the parable.

> WHERE YOUR TREASURE IS, THERE ALSO IS YOUR HEART.

Imagine the joy of the person who stumbled upon such a treasure. Upon discovering it, he/she joyfully sold all they had to buy the field and take the treasure home. Jesus challenged his disciples to seek the kindom with that same spirit . . . joyfully, eagerly, willing to forsake all else for his sake and the sake of the reign of God he held out to them.

The second parable likened the reign of God to a Pearl of Great Price (Matthew 13:45-46). In this story a person of means, a jewel merchant, was searching for the single most valuable commodity in the ancient world, a pearl. Some ancient writers claimed that fine pearls were valued more highly than gold. When one pearl of such great value was found, the merchant liquidated all of his/her assets and bought it. What a risk, you may be inclined to think . . . but this is precisely the point of the parable. More important than what is forsaken is that which is found! As T. Manson has explained, those who find the treasure of the reign of God have found a "wealth which devalues all other currencies." When a believer is blessed with the discovery of that reign, no risk is too great, no investment is too costly. There can be no half- measures and no holding back; commitment must be total and unreserved.

Another parable which underscores this idea of risking all and investing everything for the sake of the supreme value of God's reign is the parable of the Talents or Silver Pieces (Matthew 25:14-30). Before leaving on a journey, a wealthy employer called in three employees and entrusted some funds to each. Each was allotted capital in accord with their capabilities: one was entrusted with ten silver pieces, another with five and a third with one. Two of the employees worked hard, invested and doubled their money; the other chose the easy way out.

Taking no chances, the one who had received one silver piece dug a hole and buried the money. After a long absence, the employer returned to settle accounts with the employees. The two who doubled their money received the same reward: their employer's praise, a greater degree of responsibility and an invitation to share in an intimate friendship with their employer. But the third employee, who feared failure and allowed that fear to lead to inactivity, was cast out.

The lesson here is a powerful one. In spite of the fear of failure, in spite of the risks and uncertainties, believers are called to "spend" or to "invest" the *entirety* of what they have been given, i.e., time, talents, and treasure for the sake of the supreme value of the kindom. As J.P. Meier has pointed out, this parable illustrates "the basic law of the interaction between God's free gift and human response." A disciple who gives himself or herself fully to the gift God has given will receive even greater gifts, the greatest of those being the reign of God itself! But the person who plays it safe, and who expends little or none of the gifts which God has given, will receive nothing further and eventually will lose even the little that they have.

This parable, like every other parable Jesus told, presents its reader, whether of the first or 20th century, with a challenge. Each parable, every time it is read, necessitates a response, a response which is joyful but not naive, a response which is free but not careless, a response which is brave but not foolhardy. Every parable is a wonderful and unique opportunity for the believer to grow in the knowledge of Jesus, to experience the power of God's reign and to deepen in his/her loving and faithful commitment to God and to others.

Reflections

1. What are you willing to risk for the sake of the reign of God?

2. Have you ever "dug a hole" so as not to risk your time, your talent and your treasure?

Family

CHAPTER ONE

ThE NESTiNq GROuNd of SOCiETy ANd ThE CHuRCH

In one of her rare personal interviews, the recently deceased Jacqueline Kennedy Onassis remarked: "If you bungle raising your children, I don't think whatever else you do well matters very much" (quoted in *Good Housekeeping*, July 1994). For a woman whose wealth, education, background and connections could have assured her a prestigious career in academia, politics or diplomacy, the statement may seem surprising. But Mrs. Kennedy was convinced that family was ultimately the most important element in her life; as history will attest, she lived by that conviction.

Mrs. Kennedy was aware that the human family is the place where values and virtues grow. Because of its special focus on the future generation, healthy families are essential and play a unique and central role in contributing toward the well-being of society. However, during the past quarter-century a variety of factors have contributed to the progressive fragmentation, isolation and the structural evolution of the family unit. Commenting on the growing complexity of the situation of the contemporary family, legal expert Arthur Miller stated that in the past, the subject of family law could be covered in one to one-and-one-half days at any reputable school of law. Today, however, the issues and circumstances of family living have become so complex as to warrant an entire course on the subject.

Not immune from the world in which they live, Christian families have borne the brunt of such changes and have been equally affected by: (1) an ever-increasing divorce rate (there are more than one million divorces per year in the U.S.; one-third of all school-aged children do not live with both parents); (2) a steady rise in the number of one-parent households (23.1% among whites, 62.5% among blacks, 33.1% among Hispanics); (3) an increased number of families in which both parents must seek employment outside the home (more than 50% of all households); (4) a substantial number of unmarried couples or unrelated adults living together; (5) mobility (20% of American families change their residence annually; this weakens the ties of the extended family and decreases community identity).

These factors are compounded by an increasingly secularized environment in which certain segments of the political machine, the media and advertising are either indifferent to the plight of the family or are promoting values which militate against its integrity.

Aware of the situation of the contemporary human family and sympathetic to its needs, the participants at the Second Vatican Council affirmed,

> The family is the principal school of the social virtues which are necessary to every society. It is above all in the Christian family, inspired by the grace and the responsibility of the sacrament of matrimony, that children should be taught to know and worship God and to love their neighbor . . . In it, they will have their first experience of a well-balanced human society and of the Church . . . It is through the family that children are gradually initiated into association with their fellow human beings in civil life and as members of the people of God. (*Declaration on Christian Education*, #3, 28 October 1965)

If, therefore, the family is both the nesting ground and proving ground for society and for the church, its contributions are invaluable. Perhaps the first and foremost contribution a healthy family can give to each of its members is a strong sense of self and a reverence for oneself as a unique irrepeatable gift of God. According to experts

> THOSE WHO GROW UP IN THE AWARENESS OF BEING LOVED BECOME THE LOVING ADULTS OF THE NEXT GENERATION.

in the field of human development (viz. Dr. Benjamin Spock and Dr. Terry Brazelton), it is during the first two to three years of life that children's personalities are most actively molded by the attitudes of their parents and/or other significant adults who care for them. This being so, it is of the utmost importance that children be welcomed with unconditional and constant love. "Made in the image and likeness of God" (Genesis 1:26), these small, helpless and dependent beings are, from the moment of their conception, entrusted by their Creator-Father to the stewardship (not ownership) of human hands and hearts. The loving concern, caring and secure matrix within which the child is received and nurtured will greatly influence the capacity of that child to love, care and nurture others:

> Even before life begins (when one considers the act of love from which life can occur) and most certainly after life has begun to be, life must be preserved. The future of life is inseparable from the reverence with which we honor the life we have and from the history of life as it goes its way in hope (Anthony

Padovano, *Belief in Human Life*). Those who grow up in the awareness of themselves as loved and lovable become the loving adults of the next generation. Because of their rootedness in family and a healthy, holy sense of self, these adults will more readily respect and accept each person they meet regardless of race, gender, age, capability, culture, etc. If growing human beings are loved and valued as gifts, regardless of any physical, mental, developmental or emotional challenges they may have, then they are empowered to become fully and freely all that God has intended them to be. To devalue or reject another because of differences which have been perceived by society as handicaps or "abnormalities" is to devalue and to reject the mysterious and wondrous workings of God among God's people.

> REVERENCE FOR life ANd A STRONG SENSE Of SElf AS lovAblE, uNiQuE ANd vAluAblE ARE gifTS which wE ARE privilEgEd ANd RESPONSiblE fOR giviNg TO ONE ANOTHER.

When the authors of the Hebrew Scriptures wrote:

I give you thanks, Lord, that I am so wonderfully made . . . it was you who created my inmost self, and put me together in my mother's womb; for all these mysteries I thank you . . . for the wonder of myself, for the wonder of your works . . . You have made me little less than a god, you have crowned me with glory and splendor (Psalm

139:8; Ecclesiastes 11:5; Wisdom 7:1; Job 10:10), there were no stipulations or qualifying remarks as to physical or mental capabilities, no conditions with regard to freedom of choice, convenience, limitation of family size, economic situation, etc. There is simply gratitude and wonder for the amazing graciousness of a loving God who blesses all people with life and endows them with the dignity of participating in and preserving every sacred aspect of that life.

When the authors of the Christian Scriptures shared their perception of Jesus and of the values by which he lived, they offered a vision of a man who reverenced men, women and children as well as the marital and familial bonds which bound them to one another in love. Moreover, Jesus revealed himself as a brother and a Son of a loving God who longed to welcome home, *without exception*, all who desired a place in his eternal family. In accord with the mind of Jesus, Paul reminded his contemporaries, *and us*, of the value and dignity accorded each of us by God . . . in letting us be called *children* of God, in making us *temples* of the Holy Spirit, in calling us to become *new men* and *new women* in Christ who died for us while we were still sinners (Romans).

Reverence for life and a strong sense of self as lovable, unique and valuable to both God and humanity is a basic and necessary gift; it is a gift which each of us is both privileged and responsible for giving, not simply to children, but also to one another as members of the human family on this planet. Husbands and wives give this gift to each other by the mutual love and reverence they share; grandparents, grandchildren, aunts, uncles, nieces, nephews, godparents and friends, all are called upon to foster in one another that sense of self without which holiness and wholeness cannot be attained. John Henry Cardinal Newman (1801-1890), a British Anglican church leader who converted to Roman Catholicism and was made a cardinal by Pope Leo XIII, described this special sense of self in the following words:

God has created me to do him some definite service; He has committed some work to me which he has not committed to another. I have my mission . . . I am a link in a chain, a bond of connection between persons. Therefore, I will trust him. Whatever, wherever I am, I can never be thrown away. If I am in sickness, my sickness may serve him; if I am in sorrow, my sorrow may serve him. He does nothing in vain; He knows what he is about.

Reflections

1. Do you agree with Jacqueline K. Onassis' remark about raising children?

2. How has the definition of family evolved since the last century?

3. Do you think family values have improved or declined? Why?

Chapter Two

Handing on the Heritage of the Faith

In the years following the Second Vatican Council, the worldwide community of Catholics experienced a wave of renewal. For some, the changes initiated by the Council's participants seemed like a tidal wave which swept away all they had known, leaving their lives like a beach at low tide, strewn with the shells of a former way of life; for others, the renewal was welcomed like the tide which swells to the shoreline, bringing with it new life as well as new possibilities and opportunities for venturing into the future.

Perhaps one of the more readily perceptible aspects of the Council's efforts was the renewed emphasis on the fuller participation of the faithful in the worship of the Church, viz. in the liturgy and sacraments. Also affirmed was the primary role of parents in the relig-

> **Parents are the primary educators and catechists (faith-sharers) of their children.**

ious education and growth in the life of faith of their children.

Parents should appreciate how important a role the truly Christian family plays in the life and progress of the whole people of God. Christian couples are for each other, for their children and for their relatives, cooperators of grace and witnesses of the faith. They are the first to pass on the faith to their children and to educate them in it. By word and example they form them to a Christian and apostolic life. By the mutual affection of its members and by family prayer, the family presents itself as a domestic sanctuary of the Church. If the whole family takes part in the Church's liturgical worship, if the family offers active hospitality and practices justice and other good works for the benefit of all those suffering from want, its God-given mission will be accomplished. (*Declaration on Christian Education*, #3; *Decree on the Apostolate of the Laity*, #11)

In the years following the Second Vatican Council, bishops in all the dioceses throughout the world endeavored to increase their assistance of parents and families in shouldering their unique responsibilities for future generations of believers. Catechetical programs were developed which further educated and supported parents in their special role. Preparatory sessions for receiving the sacraments of initiation included mandatory parental participation. Indeed, in those instances in which parents or other significant adults refused to participate in the catechetical and/or sacramental preparation of their children, pastors were free to exercise their prerogative of delaying the reception of the sacraments. Without familial involvement and the assurance that the child's faith life and ability to participate in the liturgical life of the Church would continue, the mere reception of the sacrament left the child like a tree without roots and a bird without wings. Just as parents are uniquely influential in endowing their children with a strong sense of self and a reverence for their life as a unique gift of God, so also are parents fundamentally indispensable for the wholesome and holy development of their child's faith.

From the moment a loving couple becomes aware that a child will be borne to them, they begin earnest preparations for that child's future. The necessities of life (food, shelter, clothing), as well as all the amenities the family can possibly afford, are provided, gladly and proudly. Bank accounts are padded to secure an education and to protect against unforeseen exigencies. Wills are revised to assure the future inheritance of the child. But there is an inheritance far more valuable and enduring which the parents are privileged to impart: the rich heritage of the faith.

More than a body of knowledge, more than mere intellectual assent to a book or a creed, faith is a lived response to the call of God; it is that way of living which seeks to encounter God and God's will in all things, in all events, and which alone can find meaning in life, with all its joys, challenges, mysteries and sufferings. Faith is the willingness to stand daily in the presence of God and to say "yes" to God's summons. If parents live in such a manner, even without a word, their silent witness will speak volumes about the centrality of God as the source, guide and goal of all human life. So, too, the parents' participation together (or separately if their religious affiliations differ) in the prayer life and activities of their church community will be an invaluable and formative example for their children.

Statistics gathered in the preparation of the National Catechetical Directory (*Sharing the Light of Faith*, November 1977), indicated that, while mothers are usually the primary caretakers of their child's catechetical formation (teaching prayers, helping with homework, chauffeuring to and from school, C.C.D., religious programs), re-

> Those who are nurtured with love and care are more able to comprehend the heart and mind of our gracious God.

markably, it is the father of the family whose faith (or lack thereof) has the more profound and long-term influence on the child and on the development of his/her faith and spirituality.

A gift which begins in the womb and survives even to the grave, the faith-filled home also provides a matrix in which the child will develop his/her initial concept of God. Those who are nurtured by loving, caring parents and siblings will more ably understand and relate to God as loving Parent and to Jesus as Son and Brother. Those who grow up in the knowledge that God loves them beyond measure, knows their needs, hears their prayers, and always forgives will approach God more easily and freely as adolescents and adults. Conversely, those who are threatened, albeit without malice, with the fearful idea that God keeps track of their failures and is "going to get them" when they misbehave, will grow up with a distorted view of God. Similarly, those whose religious initiation is ignored or postponed, "so that the child may choose his/her religious orientation when old enough to do so," are poorly attended by those to whom they have been entrusted by God.

Another aspect of the faith heritage which parents can give to their children can be imparted through prayer. Grace before and after meals, scripture reading, the family rosary, morning offerings and night prayers, parental blessings for children, etc. . . . all of these can awaken even in the preverbal child the desire and appreciation for that prayerful communion with God which remains a lifelong habit. It is a well-documented and generally accepted fact that children who are accustomed to having their parents read to them become better readers and more avid learners. Cannot the same principle apply to the custom of family prayer?

By way of summation, perhaps the following amusing anecdote best illustrates the profound influence of parental example upon the life and faith of a young believer:

> On a very hot and humid day, a family was entertaining guests for dinner. When all were seated, the father asked his six-year-old son to say the prayer before the meal. "But Daddy, I don't know what to say," he protested. "Oh, just say what you've heard me say," the mother said. Obediently, the boy bowed his little head and said, "Oh Lord, why did I invite all these people here on a hot day like this!"

Reflections

1. What is the most important thing you learned from your parents about your faith?

2. What is the most important thing you would like to hand on to your children? nieces? nephews?

CHAPTER THREE

VALUES, MORAL DEVELOPMENT, CONSCIENCE

In one of his recent books, the former U.S. Secretary of Education, Dr. William J. Bennett, observed:

> We have ceased being clear about the standards we hold and the principles by which we judge. As a result, we have suffered a cultural breakdown of sorts, in areas like education, family life, crime, and drug abuse, as well as in our attitudes toward sex, individual responsibility, civic duty and public service. (*The De-Valuing of America: The Fight for Our Culture and Our Children*, Summit Books: 1992)

Among the several reasons for this lack of clarity and the resulting cultural disintegration are: (1) the ever-changing circumstances faced by the modern family, e.g., divorce, separation, economic tensions, mobility, decreased contact with relatives, lack of communication, and time spent together, etc.; (2) the "information superhighway" has had a decided effect on standard family life rituals. At the turn of this century it was the telephone, then came radio, motion pictures, television, computers, electronic games, and now virtual reality. *All of these media are good in themselves*, but if they detract from or replace the time which families need to grow both together and as individuals, they offer only a disservice; (3) "Mixed messages" have also served to confuse and bewilder those in the process of forming and developing their values. For example, it is difficult to believe in the value of peace and the policy of nonviolence when so many attempt to solve this world's problems by war and the threat of nuclear proliferation. In a nation which pledges equal rights but tolerates discrimination, values suffer. Growing children who are taught that cooperation is a good and necessary aspect of life are also told to "look out for yourself, no one else will"!

In school, children learn about patriots who spawned our revolution by speaking their minds; they also are advised to be careful of what they say, and to go along with the status quo so as not to "rock the boat" and to get ahead. They learn that education is a great value which enriches life; but the child is also apt to learn that it is the *symbols* of education, e.g., the diploma or the degree, which are truly important. They are schooled in the necessity of knowledge and the development of personal skills and talents, and are also told that it is "not *what* you know but *who* you know that really counts."

Religion and faith are offered as desirable and wholesome aspects of life, but the child also learns that religion "shouldn't interfere with politics or business." On the one hand, children are taught that life is a precious and sacred gift, and on the other they see that when a life is deemed to be inconvenient or when it is considered to be of lesser "quality" because of handicaps, age, grave sickness or pain, it is acceptable to end it.

In sports, children are taught that what truly counts is "not whether you win or lose, but how you play the game," and yet they see a soccer player murdered because he was blamed for the fact that his country lost their bid in the World Cup. If *people* are truly of more value than *things*, how is it that there are so many incidents of young people being robbed and killed for their designer clothes or shoes?

With these and so many other inconsistencies, it becomes increasingly difficult for contemporary children to develop clear values and make wise decisions. This being the case, it is not surprising that the *24th Annual Who's Who Among American High School Students Survey* (1992-1993) reports that 80% of the respondents said cheating was common in their schools, and 78% said they had also cheated. A Louis Harris survey of Girl Scouts in 1989 discovered that 21% of elementary and 51% of junior high students said they cheated. In a 1992 Roper Organization survey, a large group of 18 to 29-year-olds were asked what they considered to be the most important factors for getting ahead in the world: 89% answered "Who you know," 69% responded "playing politics," while 39% admitted that "deceit" and "corruption" would also factor into their success.

> **Values and the clarification of values, healthy moral development and the formation of a correct conscience are the primary responsibility of the family.**

Faced with such an assessment, some might be tempted to throw up their hands in discouragement, but as Christians we are called to move beyond discouragement to determination. Values and the clarification of one's values, healthy moral development and the formation of a correct conscience are the primary responsibility of the Christian family. Subsequent formation, affirmation and the continued support of each person's values, morals and conscience must be the concern of the entire Christian community.

In the Hebrew Scriptures, parents are reminded that *they* have been summoned by God to teach their children "the commandments, the laws and customs" of God (Deuteronomy 6:1-4), and to teach not only by the words they speak but also by the living example they give (Deuteronomy 6:5-19). When children have both heard and observed the integrity by which their parents live, they will then begin to question the motivation which inspired such a way of life (Deuteronomy 6:20). At that point they shall be ready to listen and to learn of the ways of the Lord for them (Deuteronomy 6:21-25). At that point, they will be prepared to understand that the Ten Commandments are not "suggestions," and that right and wrong are not relative terms but distinct realities which demand reasoned and moral choices.

In the Israelite Sapiential or Wisdom literature, the book of Proverbs (especially chapters 2-8) is replete with practical advice with regard to those values and principles by which a believer should live. Repeatedly, the Hebrew sages advise young people to "seek wisdom" by "heeding a father's instruction" and by "paying close attention to a mother's teaching." Those who seek wisdom will also enjoy the serendipitous discovery of truth,

> Mixed MESSAGES confuse and muddle the minds of those who are forming and developing values.

lucidity of thought, perception, integrity, sound judgment, virtue, honor and life! (Proverbs 8:12-21, 32-36).

Significantly, the authors of the Christian Scriptures realized that the presentation of Wisdom in the Old Testament was foundational for understanding Jesus. As the incarnate Wisdom of God, Jesus, in his person and in his mission, remains the ultimate source and teacher of values and morals (1 Corinthians 1:24, John 6:35ff). Parents who personally introduce their children to Jesus and to the challenge of the good news, and who witness to the importance of Christ and the gospel in their own lives are thereby laying a firm foundation for the moral development of the next generation. These young believers are called to "put on the mind of Christ" (Philippians 2:5), and to allow their relationship with him to permeate their words, works, thoughts, decisions and choices; in this way they will offer to the world not a mixed message which confuses but a consistent and wholesome standard of excellence.

Reflections

1. What are some of the mixed messages you have perceived in society?
2. Suggest ways in which parents might deal with society's seemingly contradictory influence on their children.

CHAPTER FOUR

AM I MY BROTHER'S/SISTER'S KEEPER?

Over the past several years, those who present the daily telecasts of current events have developed a policy of prefacing certain news items with the statement, "We should warn you that some of the film footage you are about to see could be disturbing." What follows are usually scenes of suffering people, victimized by war, prejudice, famine, disease or catastrophes of nature (flood, drought, earthquake, etc.). While those who offer such cautions may be motivated by concern for the sensibilities of the viewing public, their statements are symptomatic of a profound problem in human society, viz., our inattentiveness and even indifference to the needs of others. Frequently, the commercials which follow such a warning and the "disturbing" televised report feature a diet remedy for the self-in-

> REGARdLEss of how diligENTly WE MAY ATTEMpT TO immuNiZE ourSElVES AGAiNST THE pliGHT of oTHERS, WE wHo cAll ourSElVES CHRisTiAN ARE NOT fREE TO do so.

dulgent or a "cherished" cat eating tasty morsels of food out of a crystal compote.

While such contrasting presentations virtually scream out for rectification, they often pass before our eyes without registering with our head or our heart. Regardless of how diligently human beings may attempt to inure or immunize themselves against the plight of others, we who call ourselves Christian may not do so. I am, indeed, my brother's and my sister's keeper.

A sense of responsibility for others is another of the necessary gifts which nurturing families impart to one another. In fact, concern for others and the willingness to translate that concern into active service follows in a natural progression when one develops a holy and wholesome sense of self, a sense of God, and a moral conscience.

Basic to the development of a social consciousness is the *value* which we place on other human beings. In his excellent book, *The Power of Myth*, Joseph Campbell observed:

> The Indians addressed all of life as a "thou" . . . if you address another as a "thou" you can feel the change in your psychology. The ego that sees a "thou" is not the same ego that sees an "it."

In other words, we are to cherish others as divinely loved and blessed members of the Body of Christ and to value each person's unique contribution to the human community. Of course, our model in all our interactions should be Jesus himself, who summoned believers to "love one another as I have loved you," and who then proceeded to manifest that love without discrimination, without measure, and without seeking reciprocation.

Some may suggest that today's world is far more complex than that of Jesus' time, and that this complexity has spawned a number of obstacles which prohibit such an ideal (some would say *unrealistic* and *impractical*) life-style. But Jesus' world also had its complexities. Well-defined and enforced religious and social mores prohibited the association of "good" or "upright" people with those regarded as unworthy. Some biblical scholars have called these mores or rules the "maps" of a society which legislate order and right. Even a cursory survey of the gospels will reveal the fact that Jesus redefined the religious and social mores of his society and redrew the "maps," thereby including among the predilect of God's kingdom sinners, foreigners, tax collectors, outcasts, lepers, cripples, the possessed, and every other marginal group.

After Jesus' resurrection, the community of believers who followed his teachings continued to make his social consciousness their own. As is illustrated in the letters of the New Testament and in *Acts of the Apostles*, the early Church's continuous attentiveness and service to those in need was not developed without difficulty. Throughout the centuries this struggle has been a major aspect of the Church's contribution to the worldwide community. Today, relief programs and community services are organized on a global scale, but the roots for such efforts must begin in each Christian family.

Parents automatically begin to foster such attitudes of love among their children when they: (1) teach their infants and toddlers to share their toys with their siblings and friends; (2) coax the child to give one of her cookies to another or to share part of his apple; (3) ask their child to include others in their games; (4) advise their child not to ridicule or to exclude a child who is different or otherwise exceptional. These practices are understood as integral to the healthy socialization of youngsters.

Parents can also, by word and example, form their children to a Christian and apostolic life.

Among the various works of the family apostolate are the following: (1) adopting abandoned children; (2) showing a loving welcome to strangers; (3) helping with the running of schools; (4) supporting adolescents with advice and help; (5) assisting engaged couples to make better preparation for marriage; (6) taking a share in religious education or catechetics; (7) supporting married people and families in a material or moral crisis; (8) caring for the aged by providing them with basic human needs and procuring for them a fair share of the fruits of economic progress (*Degree on Apostolate of Lay People*, 18 November 1965, #11).

As children grow into adolescence, and then to adulthood, their social parameters become much more extensive and comprehensive. So also must their social concerns. At this point in their children's social development, many families look for support from church groups and organizations. If these various groups are to function as authentic extensions of the Church, their concerns and activities should be reflective of the Church's mandate, which was enunciated by the participants of the Second Vatican Council as follows:

The joy and hope, the grief and anguish of the people of our time, especially of those who are poor or afflicted in any way, are the joy and hope, the grief and anguish of the followers of Jesus Christ as well . . . The social order and its development must constantly yield to the good of the person. Therefore, the social order requires constant improvement; it must be founded in truth, built on justice and enlivened by love. It should grow in freedom towards a more human equilibrium. If these objectives are to be attained, there will first have to be a renewal of attitudes and far-reaching social changes. The Spirit of

God, who with wondrous providence directs the course of time and renews the face of the earth, assists in this development. The Gospel has aroused and continues to arouse in the hearts of all persons an unquenchable thirst for human dignity. (*Pastoral Constitution on the Church in the Modern World*, 7 December 1965, #4, 26).

In order to realize this mandate, various church groups, such as Y.C.S., C.Y.O., Scout organizations, and others affiliated with the parishes, should include service projects and other ministries along with their sports and recreational activities. As a result of their increased involvement in the service aspect of the community, young people will mature with a greater sense of identity with the Church, as well as a sense of responsibility for its mission to the world.

Parents can also foster their children's social consciousness by encouraging them to develop their talents and to earn an education, not simply in terms of a prestigious or lucrative *career* but as a way of living out their *vocation* from God among God's people. In one of his many eloquent statements, Winston Churchill remarked, "We make a *living* with what we get; we make a *life* with what we give." Within each healthy and holy Christian family, the roots, fruits and flowers of the future of society are growing. "What we get" within that basic Christian community will greatly affect who we are and "what we give."

> WE MAKE A LIVING WITH WHAT WE GET; WE MAKE A LIFE WITH WHAT WE GIVE.

Reflections

1. How can you help to develop the social consciousness of your children?

2. Do you think the mandate as expressed in the *Constitution on the Church in the Modern World* (see quote above) is attainable? Why? Why not?

CHAPTER FIVE

Rules and Regulations: Leading-Strings of Love

When Hosea, the eighth-century B.C.E. prophet, called his people to remember their relationship with God and to live according to the way he had shown them, he used the image of a loving parent attempting to teach and to guide his child:

> *When Israel was a child, I loved him,*
> *and I called my son out of Egypt.*
> *But the more I called to them,*
> *the further they went from me.*
> *I myself taught Ephraim to walk*
> *I took them in my arms . . .*
> *I led them with reins of kindness,*
> *with leading-strings of love.*
> *I was like someone who lifts an infant*
> *close against his cheek;*
> *stooping down to him,*
> *I gave him his food . . .* (Hosea 11:1-5)

With such tenderness, God loved and nurtured God's people, protecting them from harm, teaching them how to walk and to become authentic and free in their response to God. In his translation of the Bible, James Moffatt (1870-1944), a Scottish minister and bible scholar, rendered "leading strings of love" as a "harness of love, and compared it to the device which parents of toddlers use to keep their little ones in check. This image reminded me of a lesson I learned years ago: My father, who was in the Air Force, had received orders for Japan, and went on ahead of us to arrange for housing, etc. My mother, younger brother and I followed a few months later. Our twelve-day trip across the Pacific abroad the *U.S.S. Edward* seemed endless to me. To make the time pass more quickly, my mother took us for daily walks on the deck of the huge ship. On each walk, my brother, who was three years old at the time, was required to wear a harness attached to a leather "leash," which my mother held securely. Regulations aboard the ship required the use of such a harness for all children under five. When I objected that it seemed "mean" to keep the youngster so constrained, my mother explained that the harness was really a good and loving thing because it assured that my brother would be kept from being swept overboard if the ship should suddenly list to one side or the other. Only years later did she tell me that some children had actually perished at sea before the harness rule was implemented.

THE NECESSARY RULES WITH WHICH PARENTS RAISE THEIR CHILDREN ARE "LEADING STRINGS OF LOVE" AND "REINS OF KINDNESS."

In a sense, both Hosea and my mother taught a similar lesson. The necessary rules and regulations with which loving parents raise their children are "leading-strings of love" and "reins of kindness," which safeguard and protect their lives and well-being as they grow to maturity and become responsible for their own actions and decisions. For Israel, these "reins" or "leading-strings" were the law or the commandments which God had given through Moses. The law or Torah was regarded as that teaching of God which, if followed, would result in the people's well-being. "My child, do not forget my teaching (*torah* = law); let your heart keep my principles, for these will give you lengthier days, longer years of life and greater happiness" (Proverbs 3:1). For Christians, the "reins" or "leading-strings of love" go further than the Torah and include a new type of discipline taught by Jesus himself.

Rules are not only for disciples but for discipling.

Discipline, from which the word *disciple* is derived, means instruction or teaching. Although today the word is generally understood to refer to punishment or control, this is not and should not be its primary meaning. Jesus' new discipline or teaching included a call to love God fully, to love one's neighbor as oneself, and to follow Jesus as a disciple, i.e., as one who is willing to be taught. In his excellent book, *Discipling in the Church*, Marlin Jeschke advises parents (teachers, ministers, etc.) to think of the rules and regulations which they impose upon their children not only as a discipline for the sake of order, but as a process of *discipling*. By these rules, parents instruct children in the ways of Christ. By word and example, parents correct and restore their children to Christ's way; by so doing, they help to assure that they will grow into moral, conscientious adults. Therefore, the goal of all parental rules should not be simply to produce well-disciplined young people, but to foster and nurture healthy and holy *disciples* of Jesus.

Obviously, the rules and regulations which parents agree upon for their children evolve and develop as the children grow from infancy to maturity. According to the Jean Piaget-Lawrence Kohlberg "schema of moral development," very young children keep the rules imposed by their parents because they wish to please them and to avoid their annoyance or displeasure. As children move toward adolescence, their attitude toward parental rules shifts: the acceptance of and a desire to conform to their peers becomes more important. It is beneficial if the adolescent has some input into the decisions concerning the rules he/she is expected to keep, as well as into the sanctions which will result when the rules are broken. At this point, there may be conflict because rules and regulations differ from household to household. So often parents hear the objection, "But, everyone is doing it!," and they begin to feel like solitary islands in a sea of permissiveness. For those who have heard the objection and felt the isolation, the words of sacred scripture offer support and encouragement. "Be strong, fear not . . . let your yes be yes and your no be no . . . parents, never drive your children to resentment but in bringing them up, correct them and guide them as the Lord does" (Isaiah 35:4, Matthew 5:37, Ephesians 6:4). There is also a lesson to be learned from a conversation overheard between two teenaged boys: One told his friend that his parents thought he was too young to date. "Oh, that's so uncool," said the friend. "My parents don't care; they let me do whatever I want." Although he probably did so unconsciously, the young teen equated a lack of *rules* with a lack of *care*. "Reins of kindness" and "leading strings" may chafe at times, but *eventually* are perceived as acts of love and signs of care by those who have experienced them.

In the more advanced stages of their moral development, mature young people begin to accept and to keep parental rules because they have become personally convinced that these both represent and protect the values by which they have decided to live. Arriving at this level of maturity is not achieved without struggle and occasional failure. But these instances of difficulty can be learning experiences which both build character and test moral principles.

Each family with its unique and special members will develop its own rules. When these are perceived as "reins of kindness" and "leading-strings of love" by those who give and by those who adhere to them, then the process of discipling moves forward and the family remains the fertile nesting ground of society and the Church.

Reflections

1. What is the best way to formulate and explain rules to children?

2. How do you cope when the rules of your household differ from other households?

Chapter Six

Security, Spirituality, Sanctity

Father Theodore Hesburgh, C.S.C., President Emeritus of Notre Dame University, once remarked: "The most important thing a father can do for his children is to love their mother." Even more important than life's basic necessities, e.g., food, clothing and shelter, is the love which binds two people together in marriage and creates a secure home in which to welcome and nurture their children. In a similar comment on the importance of a secure and happy familial atmosphere, Washington Irving wrote, "It was the policy of the good old gentleman to make his children feel that home was the happiest place in the world; and I value this delicious home-feeling as one of the choicest gifts a parent can give."

Significantly, no other living species on this planet requires between eighteen and twenty (or more) years in order to face life independently. Even when physical maturity has been achieved, human children remain with their parents. In order for their personalities and unique identities to fully mature, a protracted period of loving nurture between parents and children and their siblings is absolutely necessary. In re-

> The most important thing a father can do for his children is to love their mother.

ality, the familial bond between them is never broken; it remains all through life and imparts a sense of security and stability in an often otherwise unfriendly and unstable world. Within the "delicious" atmosphere of a healthy family, we make our first discoveries of ourselves, of God and others.

When parents wish to impart a sense of their unique identity to their children, they often employ the image of a family tree, which includes as many relatives for as many generations as can be traced. To understand one's place within the structure of the family tree is to know *who I am* and from *where I came*. Parents may point out to children their resemblance to an aunt, uncle or grandfather. Personality traits and particular talents for art, music, math, etc., are similarly attributed to familial ancestry. All of these roots and relationships form a secure matrix within which healthy people develop and from which they derive the gift of happy, formative memories. This sort of exercise is particularly interesting here in the United States, where most Americans can eventually trace their ancestry to other countries.

> Each family instills in its members a sense of ethnic or ancestral identity; so should family be the place where spiritual identity is recognized and developed.

For those who believe, there is another family tree, as well as a spiritual ancestry with which to identify. Because of the infinite goodness of our Creator, we are privileged to relate to God as beloved *children* of a loving Parent. We are *brothers* and *sisters* of the Son, who gave his life that we may live. We are also *kin* to every other believer in both the Hebrew and Christian traditions. Our ancestry is cosmic; our family tree springs eternal.

Just as each family instills in its members a sense of its *ethnic* or *ancestral* identity, so should the family be the place where *spiritual* identity is recognized and developed. In their pastoral letter, *Human Life in Our Day*, the American bishops explained: *For the believer, the family is the place where God's image is reproduced in creation. The family is the community within which each person is realized, the place where all our hopes for the future of the person are nourished. The family is a learning experience in which fidelity is fostered, hope imparted and life honored; it thus increases the moral resources of our culture and, more importantly, of the person. The family is a sign to all humanity of fidelity to life and of hope in the future which becomes possible when persons are in communion with one another; it is a sign to believers of the depth of this fidelity and this hope when these center on God; it is a sign to Christians of the fidelity and hope which Christ communicates as the elder brother of the family of the Church for which he died.*

Pledging themselves to "cooperate in multiplying ways and means toward the renewal of the family," the bishops, in conjunction with Pope John Paul II, have stressed the importance of a sound family spirituality. *Spirituality*, a term which many may suppose applies solely to the clergy and religious within the Church, has to do with *every* believer's way of being religious. Each of us, by virtue our baptism, "are to live according to the

Spirit" (Romans 8:5); we are to be consciously aware of, in touch with and motivated by that principle of life which transcends us. To be spiritual means to live according to the knowledge that God is present to us in grace. To be open to God's Holy Spirit is to acknowledge who we are and who we are called to become, and to direct our lives accordingly. As Christians, this means that we are to cultivate a life-style which is consonant with the Spirit of the Risen Christ within us and with our status as members of the Body of Christ.

All too frequently parents may be inclined to relegate the responsibility for the spirituality of their children to the Catholic school or C.C.D. program. But even in the best of circumstances, the religious education and formation in spirituality offered by such programs can only be regarded as auxiliary and subordinate to that guidance which parents alone can give. Given the fact that during the 13 years from kindergarten through high school, a child spends 16,380 hours at school (7 hours a day), 37,960 hours asleep (8 hours a day), and 59,540 hours at home or elsewhere, it devolves upon parents to assume the *primary* responsibility for their children's spirituality.

Family prayers, inspired by and geared toward participation in the weekly liturgy and liturgical seasons, provides a framework for spiritual growth and expression. Other devotions, such as scripture reading, the family rosary, morning and evening prayers, grace at meals, celebrations of feast days, baptismal days or name days (patron saint for whom child is named), all help to enrich and to express the growing faith of family members. Moreover, those unique traditions which each family develops for its own become a source of spiritual vitality for future generations. Those who pray together and celebrate the faith they share contribute to the personal *sanc-*

tity or *holiness* of each member of the family. Those who are aware of themselves as temples of the Holy Spirit will be less inclined to desecrate themselves by using illicit drugs, alcohol, cigarettes or poor dietary habits. Those who have learned reverence for themselves and for the family will be less likely to engage in premarital sex, extramarital affairs or abortion. Those with an understanding of their own personal sanctity will probably not be attracted by the pollution of pornography or random senseless violence. Those who have understood the dignity they possess as graced persons and valued members of a loving family will be less likely to be swayed by the allure of gangs, New Age gurus, cultist groups, and "psychic friends."

As we approach the third Christian millennium, the family will be a necessary and vital force for goodness. To that end, the American bishops have called the Christian family to fulfill its preeminent and prophetic mission for the world. "More now than ever, the Christian family is called to be a prophetic witness to the primacy of life. Christian families are called to confront the world with the full reality of human love and proclaim to the world the mystery of divine love as these are revealed through the family."

Reflections

1. How can you help to develop the spirituality of your children?

2. Is this a responsibility you think you can handle? Why? Why not?

The Shared Meal

CHAPTER ONE

AN ESSENTIAL HUMAN EVENT

In the earliest (ca. 53-54 C.E.) scriptural account of the Last Supper we read,

> For this is what I received from the Lord and in turn passed on to you: that on the same night that he was betrayed, the Lord Jesus took some bread, and thanked God for it and broke it, and he said, "This is my body which is for you; do this as a memorial of me." In the same way he took the cup after supper and said, "This cup is the new covenant in my blood. Whenever you drink it, do this as a memorial of me." (1 Corinthians 11:23-25)

> **MEAL SHARING IS AN ESSENTIAL ASPECT OF HUMAN SOCIETY AND AN INTEGRAL PART OF OUR MOST PROFOUND RELIGIOUS EXPERIENCE.**

Of all the possible settings he could have chosen, Jesus elected to reveal himself and the mystery of his saving mission within the context of a meal. Within the context of that shared meal, he took bread and wine and identified himself with it. At that moment, what had been a simple meal became a sacred event wherein his followers

135

would thereafter celebrate his death and continue to experience his real and saving presence.

For his contemporaries, the shared meal provided a rich and fitting matrix for understanding Jesus' words and actions, because meals were an important and central aspect of Israelite society. But as Tad Guzie, S.J., has noted, "Much of the rich meaning of the Last Supper is foreign to the modern mind because we have so little experience of the richness or depth of symbolism that can be given to a simple meal shared together." Technological advances, economic exigencies, sociological crises in family life and in marital relationships have done much to erode the time we spend together at meals, as well as the manner in which we share them. Because of this, many in our modern society lack a fundamental foundation for understanding the Eucharist as "the summit toward which the activity of the Church is directed and the fountain from which all her power flows" (Constitution on the Sacred Liturgy, #10).

The meaning of the Eucharist as a sacred, sacrificial meal is not easy to communicate to people whose daily meals lack all ritual . . . meals, which except for Thanksgiving or weddings or birthdays, amount to little more than eating and running. Breakfast eaten standing over the sink, or a sandwich eaten while driving to one's next appointment . . . these sometimes unavoidable necessities do little to foster a sense of community, which is integral to the shared meal experience. Religious educators have found that if they can foster the faithful observance of the shared meal among those whom they teach, then catechesis of the Eucharist is greatly facilitated.

Jeff Smith, an ordained Methodist minister and master chef on public television's *Frugal Gourmet* program, attributes the modern attitude toward meals to our Puritan background and the belief that the only real value in our culture is to be found in work. Accordingly, time at the table is considered time wasted or mere self-indulgence.

When the first fast-food restaurant opened in New York in 1895, business people, steeped in the Puritan work-ethic, stopped at The Exchange Buffet to stand and eat a quick meal from a long table. Less than 60 years later, the now-familiar golden arches began to appear on the American horizon, and today fast food is a world-wide phenomenon. But even fast food can provide an occasion for an authentic shared meal if those who share it allow expediency to give way to communion.

As we explore the ritual of the shared meal and trace this special event through human history, we shall find a wealth of information in the Hebrew and Christian scriptures. Therein the meal is featured as an elemental aspect of human society and as an integral part of our most profound religious experience.

According to statistics compiled at the end of the last century, during a lifetime of 70 years an average person would probably spend twenty years working, twenty years sleeping, seven years playing, five years dressing, three years waiting, one year on the telephone, two and one-half years smoking, two and one-half years resting or napping, one and one-half years in church, one year of miscellaneous activity, five months tying shoes and six years at meals. Therefore, roughly 8.5%, or a very significant portion of an average life, would have been spent at the table.

Long before history was ever recorded and long before language was fully developed, humanity nurtured itself and celebrated its existence over food. Once fire became a useful friend rather than a feared enemy, the hearth came into being. Archaeological discoveries, in the Durance valley in France, date the hearth, or human-

SHARED MEALS CREATE, CONFIRM AND CELEBRATE OUR MOST IMPORTANT RELATIONSHIPS.

made fires for cooking, as early as 750,000 years ago. Because it enabled the *communal* preparation and sharing of food, the hearth did much to make primeval humanity more social beings.

Through the centuries, meals became central events in human life, celebrating innumerable occasions, both religious and secular. Harvests, births, the changing seasons, weddings and even funerals were made more memorable by shared meals. According to the historian Herodotus, birthday feasts were a well-established custom among the ancient Persians. In *The Iliad*, the eighth-century B.C.E. poet Homer wrote of a funeral feast (the first wake?) which King Priam held for his slain son, Hector. By the fourth century C.E., meals had become such special events in the Roman empire that good cooks were revered as only slightly less than the gods. In his cookbook, Apicius documented the Roman penchant for extravagance with his menus for 22-course meals and such delicacies as nightingales' tongues, ostrich brains and pulverized pearls!

Today, our menus bear little resemblance to the Roman feasts, but the principle of the shared food is essentially the same. Food is one of the most widespread material expressions of our social interaction. We offer food when we can't find words to speak our feelings. To those mourning the death of a loved one, our offering of food and the care with which it was prepared speak a silent message of sympathy and support. And, when we *do* have words, our gift of food affirms them. A gift of food can say, "Sorry you aren't feeling well" or "Welcome to the neighborhood" or "Congratulations on the new baby!" When the gift of food is shared *together*, that sharing constitutes a meal, a human event intended to create, to confirm and to celebrate relationships.

A remarkable form of human activity, shared meals have their own special solemnity. In his book, *Sacraments for Secular Man*, George McCauley explained that true participation at meals requires a special element of communication (not always verbal) and a special attentiveness. Both of these qualities, communication and attentiveness, require the momentary putting aside of our own agenda to recognize others' needs. Those needs could be as simple as needing the salt or help in cutting food, as in the case of a child, handicapped or elderly person. There is also the need to be included in the conversation, and the need to be recognized and affirmed as an important member of the family or group. As food and drink provide physical nourishment, the communication and mutual attentiveness of the meal-sharers provide essential emotional, psychological and spiritual nourishment as well. Within the framework of this profound human experience, Jesus gave to his disciples his very self. As we better appreciate the human meal, we shall better understand and appreciate the great gift of our saving Lord.

Reflections

1. Is meal sharing an important part of your day? your life?

2. What are the most memorable and/or significant meals you have shared?

3. Do you think meal-sharing is important for understanding the Eucharist? Why?

Chapter Two

The Jewish Experience

Since the first *kibbutz* or collective settlement was founded in Deganya, Palestine in 1909, the life-style and mutual sharing among *kibbutz* members has had an ever-growing and continuing appeal. Today in modern Israel, there are over 200 of these *kibbutzim* or settlements. Jews come from all over the world to experience the democratic and egalitarian character of *kibbutz* life. All goods are shared in common; all work together in the collective's farm or factory. Parenting the children of the *kibbutz* is a responsibility shared by all adult members. There are private quarters for each family in the *kibbutz*, but all meals are prepared and shared together in a large central building. The common dining hall as the very heart of the *kibbutz* is a 20th-century development; the custom of the shared meal is a centuries' old Jewish tradition.

> **Those who share bread and salt are thereby covenanted to one another forever.**

In the ancient near-Eastern world, people did not eat together *casually* because the very act of sharing food with another was regarded as a sacred ritual; those who ate together were thereafter bound to one another in a special relationship, called a covenant. By virtue of the fact that they had shared bread and salt, they had become mutually obligated to one another, even to the point of defending the other with one's very life, should the need arise. Mutual relationships which were affirmed by shared meals were called *covenants of salt* and were regarded as *inviolable*.

In Genesis 31:54, one such covenant or agreement between Laban and Jacob was solemnized with a meal; so too in Genesis 26:15-33, the agreement over water rights between Isaac and Abimelech was confirmed by a shared meal. "We have eaten together" was a statement that was meant to convey the depth and extent of the commitment shared by two people.

So deeply rooted was the loyalty between those who had shared food together that if a thief inadvertently ate something while robbing a home, he would abandon the idea and leave the would-be victim with all his/her goods intact. Travelers in the ancient world would ensure their safe passage through dangerous regions by giving would-be robbers and/or enemies gifts of food. If they accepted and ate the food, this would preclude any violent acts against those who gave it.

So sacred was the bond created by a shared meal that those who broke the bond were considered guilty of the most serious crime. Psalm 41:9 laments such a breach of friendship: "Even my closest and most trusted friend, who shared my table, lifts his heel against me!" In the Johannine gospel, Jesus is quoted as citing this reference from Psalm 41 when foretelling Judas' betrayal (John 13:18). In light of the inviolable bond of friendship formed by shared meals, the betrayal seems all the more odious.

The Israelite concept of the mutual bond created among those who ate together also had its corollary in their religious traditions. One of the most ancient forms of sacrifice was known as the *zebah shelamim* or communion sacrifice (Leviticus 3). After an animal had been sacrificed, a portion of it, as well as the blood, was offered to Yahweh; the rest of the animal was cooked and then shared by the offerer and his/her family. The sharing of this sacrificial meal in the presence of Yahweh was thought to confirm and strengthen the union among those who shared it, as well as their union with the Lord to whom they offered it.

Because of the special character of the shared meal, hospitality was regarded as an especially sacred duty. Recall the extravagance with which Abraham and Sarah entertained the three visitors who passed by their tent at the hottest part of the day. How many of us would roast a fatted calf and bake an abundance of fresh bread for strangers who happened by at the most inopportune time of the day? But Abraham did so, only later to discover that in so doing he had actually opened his heart and home to the God he worshipped (Genesis 18; Hebrews 13:12).

Just as the ancient Israelites highly valued the ritual of shared meals, they also regarded the food itself as tangible evidence of God's provident care and as a means of experiencing God's goodness. In the mixed metaphor of Psalm 34:8, the psalmist invited the people to "*taste* and *see* the goodness of the Lord!" With a vivid description of a full table, the psalmist painted a verbal portrait of God's special care for the people, "You prepare a table before me in the sight of my enemies . . . my cup overflows" (Psalm 23:5).

Israel's sapiential or wisdom literature is lavish in its portrayal of God's goodness in banquet terminology. In the book of Proverbs, those who seek God are invited to fill themselves at Wisdom's table: "Wisdom has built herself a house . . . she has laid her table . . . Come and eat my bread, drink the wine I have prepared! Leave your folly and you will live!" (Proverbs 9:1,5-6).

Gradually, the ancient Israelites began to envision and to describe *salvation* in terms of a great banquet prepared by God for humankind. The early Christians recognized that Wisdom's table prefigured and prepared them to understand the bread of life which Jesus had prepared for humankind. Two of the most important banquet references, which help to form the basis for our understanding of Jesus' meals in the Christian scriptures, can be found in Isaiah. In Isaiah 25:6-9 and 55:1-9, all the poor peoples of the earth are invited to have their every hunger satisfied and their thirst quenched at a rich feast hosted by Yahweh. At that table, they would find the food of forgiveness and salvation, and the communion of an everlasting covenant offered freely and gratuitously by a loving, caring God.

> GRAdUAlly OUR ANCESTORS iN THE fAiTH bEGAN TO ENViSiON SAlVATiON AS A GREAT bANQUET PREPAREd by God.

Centuries later, the messianic banquet visions of Isaiah were realized in the meals which Jesus shared with his contemporaries. In the table fellowship Jesus offered, the Jewish tradition of the shared meal had come to full flower.

Reflections

1. Do you think of the Eucharist more as a shared meal or as a sacrifice?

2. Can you see how the early Christians understood Jesus as Wisdom incarnate?

Chapter Three

An Experience of Salvation

In the first Christian century, Jesus and his Jewish contemporaries celebrated formal and/or festive meals according to the custom they had adopted from the occupying forces of the Roman empire. Three beds or couches were arranged to form what was called a *triclinium*, the shape of which resembles a square minus one of its sides. The fourth side of the *triclinium* was left open so that waiters could approach and serve the guests. As they reclined, leaning on their left elbows, guests served themselves with their right hands from tables in front of each of the three couches. Usually, no more than three people occupied one couch, and all the dinner guests faced one another with their feet toward the back.

In the homes of wealthier Jews, the large dining room was left open to allow curious townspeople to pass through the room and to enjoy the table conversation of the invited guests. This would explain how the man with dropsy (Luke 14:1-6) and the sinful woman (Luke 7:36-50) could gain access to Jesus while he ate. The Roman-style dining arrangement would also explain how the woman could approach and anoint Jesus' feet while he was at table. Given such an arrangement, the gesture of the Beloved Disciple resting on Jesus' chest is more readily envisioned (John 13:23).

But the similarity between Roman dining customs and those of Jesus and his contemporaries went no further than the arrangement of the dining area. Whereas the extravagance at Roman feasts has been well-documented, little is known about the menus, guest lists, entertainment, decor, etc., at the meals which Jesus shared. Obviously, the evangelists understood that Jesus' presence was the most important element of the meal, and that all other details of the meal were subordinate to this fact.

Recall that for Jesus' contemporaries, sharing meals with others meant that those who did so were willing to form lasting bonds of friendship with their table partners. Consequently, the pious people of Jesus' day did not eat with those whom they regarded as sinners, outcasts and others outside the law. Theirs was a rigid interpretation of the law: "You must distinguish between the holy and the unholy, between the clean and the unclean" (Leviticus 10:10).

> JESUS iNCARNATEd God's ATTiTudE of wElCOME ANd ACCEPTANCE.

Joseph Fitzmyer has suggested that the Pharisees, scribes and chief priests ascribed to a principle of "salvation by segregation," i.e., out of concern for their *own* salvation they justified their shunning of others whom they regarded as outside the pale of salvation. In sharp contrast, Jesus offered a new principle: "salvation by association." By his deliberate association with sinners, the poor, outcasts, etc., Jesus offered them the experience of salvation. His presence at meals with those whom society regarded as unsaveable was a clear indication that God's ideas about salvation were decidedly different from those of the scribes and Pharisees. By his conduct at meals, Jesus incarnated the attitude of God toward humankind . . . an attitude of welcome and acceptance, *especially* for sinners. In Jesus, people learned that God wished to enter into a nourishing communion with all people and to form with them the lasting bonds of friendship.

As we read the gospels, we will notice that Jesus had a variety of table companions. In the Lucan account, for example, Jesus purposely chose to eat with two men whom the respectable members of his society shunned, viz., Levi (Luke 5:29-39) and Zaccheus (Luke 19:1-12). Both were tax collectors, i.e., Jews who worked for Rome, collecting the taxes which the empire exacted from all who lived under its domain. Levi and Zaccheus must have been fairly wealthy, because Rome required would-be tax agents to bid for the job of collecting taxes and to pay Rome, in advance, all the taxes due from their particular area. Then the collector would hire his own agents to recoup his money and make a tidy, but not always honest profit. Notorious for their greed and corruption, and despised for their cooperation with Rome, tax-collectors were considered sinners and outcasts.

Yet it was to these very people that Jesus extended the privilege and blessings of table fellowship with him. By so doing, Jesus realized and fulfilled the messianic banquet prophecies of Isaiah: *Yahweh will prepare for all peoples a banquet of rich food . . . Yahweh will wipe away the tears from every cheek, and will take away his people's shame. That day it will be said: "See, this is our God in whom we hope for salvation" . . . Come all you who are thirsty, though you have no money come . . . listen to me and your soul will live . . . Let the wicked person abandon the way of evil and turn back to our God, who is rich in forgiving!* (Isaiah 25:6-9; 55:1-9)

In the context of a shared meal, Jesus welcomed many others as well: people with diseases who were regarded as sinners and unclean (Luke 14:1-6), people with bad reputations (Luke 7:36-50), people who did not observe the cleansing rituals (Luke 11:37-54), women, who were considered lesser people and unworthy of the company of a noted rabbi or teacher (Luke 10:38-42), and crowds of people, which probably included a vast array of unclean, sinful, diseased outcasts (Luke 9:10-17). All became Jesus' table companions; all were called to salvation by association with him; all were called to welcome the reign of God made present to them in Jesus' words and works.

For each person, the call to salvation by association with Jesus entailed a conversion or change of heart. Jesus' presence at meals challenged those who accepted conversion to be nourished by him, to experience divine forgiveness and healing through him. Then each was invited to become a disciple and to affirm and seal his/her relationship with Jesus at the meal they shared.

> JESUS' PRESENCE AT SHARED MEALS CHALLENGED HIS TABLE COMPANIONS TO CONVERSION.

Reflections

1. Why was Jesus' willingness to eat with sinners so offensive to his contemporaries?

2. What is the difference between salvation by segregation and salvation by association?

CHAPTER FOUR

SALVATION FOR THE HUNGRY

Readers of the gospels will discover that Jesus frequently shared meals with those whom he met during his ministry. As a result of their sharing, those who welcomed Jesus were, in effect, welcoming salvation; they were nourished by the words and works of the very Lord of Life. But we shall also find as we read the gospels that not everyone who ate with Jesus was nourished by him. What factor enabled some to welcome Jesus, while others refused to do so?

In order to ascertain the answer to this question, it is necessary to look to the Infancy narrative, at the beginning of Luke's gospel. Within the first two chapters of his gospel, the evangelist has encapsulated, in narrative and in canticle, the entire proclamation of the good news of salvation.

The beautiful narrative of Mary's visit to Elizabeth provides the setting for Mary's canticle, known also as the *Magnificat*. Woven together within the canticle are a host of prophetic, messianic and theological themes. Although we call it *Mary's* canticle, it is actually a song about the messiah, a song of salvation. One line of the canticle proclaims, "God has filled the hungry with good things, while the rich are sent empty away" (Luke 1:53). Like all the verbs of the canticle, those in this verse are in the *prophetic perfect tense*, meaning that this is a proclamation of such certainty that it can be spoken of as having already happened!

In Jesus' actions at the meals he shared with others, the words of Mary's song were being fulfilled: the hungry were filled with good things. The hungry were being nurtured with healing, with forgiveness and with the experience of salvation. All these *good things*, formerly associated only with God (Psalm 107:9), were made available in Jesus. This fact is made quite emphatically in the Zaccheus narrative, which appears later in the Lucan gospel.

Jesus' presence in his home provided Zaccheus with the impetus for conversion. Zaccheus promised to reform his life and to make retribution, beyond what was required by law, for his wrong-doings. Jesus' words proclaimed Zaccheus' experience of salvation: "Today salvation has come to this house!" (Luke 19:9). Zaccheus, the sinful woman (Luke 7:36-50), the crowds (Luke 9:10-17), the man with dropsy (Luke 14:1-24), Levi (Luke 5:29-39) . . . all were filled with the good things Jesus had to offer because each met Jesus with the *hunger* needed to recognize and receive him. Others who shared meals with Jesus (Simon, the Pharisees, etc.,) were evidently not *hungry*. Rather, they were already *full* or *satisfied* with their own ideas of holiness, of salvation, of the Messiah. Consequently, they gave no welcome to the *good things* offered to them in Jesus; like the rich of Mary's song, they "went empty away."

> HUNGER CREATES
> THE WELCOME
> WHICH IS
> NECESSARY FOR
> BEING FED BY GOD.

When Jesus encountered this lack of hunger or self-satisfaction, while at a reception in Levi's home (Luke 5:27-39), he used the occasion to teach a powerful lesson. Criticized by the scribes and Pharisees for his association with tax collectors and sinners, Jesus declared, "I have not come to invite the self-righteous (or self-satisfied) to a change of heart, but sinners!" (Luke 5:32). He affirmed this statement with a graphic illustration: "No one pours new wine into old wineskins. If this is done, the new wine will burst the old skins . . . New wine should be poured into fresh skins!" (Luke 5:37-38).

Jesus is the new wine; his words and works, his understanding of holiness and of salvation are reflective of God's own will for humanity. But the old wineskins, or the limited and provincial matrix of Judaism (as understood by the Pharisees and scribes), could not (or would not) accept the new wine Jesus had to offer. What was needed was a new wineskin, or a new matrix, for receiving salvation. That new wineskin is hunger. Hunger creates the openness and welcome which are necessary for receiving the good news of God proclaimed in Jesus. Hunger means an awareness of need and a desire to be filled with the good things God sends in the person and mission of Jesus.

> HUNGER ENABLES THE disciple TO ATTEND TO WHAT is TRULY ESSENTIAL.

This quality of hunger is well-illustrated at the meal which Jesus shared in the home of Martha and Mary (Luke 10:42). Notice the literary context of the Mary and Martha narrative. A famed rabbi, Akiba, taught his students that God's sacred word is always better understood if one "takes note of that which stands next to it." Standing next to, i.e., immediately before, the Mary and Martha narrative is the parable of the good Samaritan (Luke 10:25-37), wherein Jesus teaches us how believers should welcome and care for their *neighbor*. At the meal he shared in Martha's home, Jesus taught how we are to welcome and care for *God*.

Martha, in her sincere effort to tend to Jesus' every need, immersed herself in the business of preparing and serving the meal. But, in the rush of hectic activity, she became too busy to hunger for the one who had come to fill her with good things. In sharp contrast, Mary represents the ideal disciple, whose hunger enabled her to understand that attentiveness to the nourishment Jesus had brought to their home was more essential.

Significantly, the Mary and Martha narrative "stands next to" another important lesson in Scripture, viz., Jesus' own prayer to God (Luke 11:1-4). In the Lord's Prayer, Jesus outlined the fundamental attitude of the believer toward God: hunger for God's reign, hunger for God's will, hunger for God-given daily bread, hunger for forgiveness and hunger for deliverance from evil. Each time we pray this prayer we renew our hunger for the good things with which God alone can fill humankind.

At most of the meals Jesus shared during his ministry, he was a guest. But in Luke 9:10-17, Jesus was the host for the crowds who had come to hear him. The meal-for-the-many, narrated in all four gospels, portrayed Jesus in the light of the messianic banquet foretold by the prophets (Isaiah 25:6-9, 55:1-9). In Jesus' generous action of providing abundant food for the crowds, God's promises to a hungry humankind were being fulfilled.

It is significant that only Luke tells us the name of the place: Bethsaida, i.e., "House of" or "Place of Satisfaction." There at Bethsaida, the words of Mary's canticle were being realized, "God has filled the hungry with good things."

When the disciples urged Jesus to send the crowds away, he challenged them, "Give them something to eat yourselves" (Luke 9:13). There, within the context of the meal for the many, we find a nascent missiology as well as a nascent ecclesiology. By his challenge to the disciples, Jesus indicated that his followers (both then and now) were to share in his mission of welcoming and feeding the hungry. Those with whom Jesus shares his meals are called to become a community (a church), the essential task or mission of which will be to nourish . . . to fill the hungry with good things.

Notice the specific words and actions with which Luke described Jesus' sharing with the crowds: "He *took* the loaves, *blessed* them, *broke* them and *gave* them . . ." (Luke 9:16). These are the same words and actions which will describe Jesus' gift of himself at the Last Supper. After Jesus' resurrection, and inspired by Easter faith, the early church understood that the meal for the many was a prelude to, and preparation for, understanding what Jesus did at the Last Supper and what the community of believers would do in memory of Jesus.

Reflections

1. When you host a shared meal, are you more like Martha or like Mary?

2. When you come to be fed at the Eucharistic table, are you more like Martha or like Mary?

3. What are the fundamental hungers which guide your life?

CHAPTER FIVE

THE LAST SUPPER-EUCHARISTIC EVENT

Shortly before his death, Jesus shared a special last meal with his disciples. Given the insight and perspective afforded them by Jesus' resurrection, the disciples recognized that the Last Supper had been both a *culmination* and a *commencement*. As the *culmination*, that sacred meal constituted the climax of all the meals Jesus had shared during his ministry. As the *commencement*, the Last Supper became the basis and the motivation for all the future meal communion to be enjoyed by Jesus and his disciples.

At the Last Supper, Jesus took bread and wine and identified himself with them. But he did not do so in a void; Jesus' actions were founded on traditions, rituals and structures which were already deeply ingrained in the life-experiences and spirituality of his contemporaries. Jesus' actions were firmly rooted in the ritual of the shared meal and in the covenantal ties and mutual obligations which the meal signified. Jesus' actions were also built upon the ritual of the Jewish Passover meal; this fact is quite evident in the synoptic gospels, especially in the Lucan version of the good news (see Luke 22:1-38).

Jesus took the bread and the wine of the Passover meal and gave them a new meaning. He reinterpreted the significance of the Passover and its symbols and he instructed his followers to repeat what he had done as a memorial of him. To understand more fully the profound meaning and significance of Jesus' actions at the Last Supper, it is necessary to appreciate the Passover ritual and its traditions.

Passover is an annual feast which remembers and celebrates the Exodus from Egypt and the subsequent relationship or covenant which God initiated with Israel in the wilderness of Sinai. Jesus and his contemporaries observed the feast according to the stipulations recorded in Exodus 12:3-14 (see parallel texts, Numbers 9:1-14, Deuteronomy 16:1-8). One of the three major pilgrimage feasts, Passover brought Jews from all over Israel and parts of the diaspora to Jerusalem. Lambs were sacrificed and their blood was poured out in praise of God, who had spared the lives of the people while they were enslaved in Egypt. With the lamb, unleavened bread was eaten as a remembrance of the escape from Egypt, when there had been no time wait for leavened bread to rise. Bitter herbs were eaten to recall the sorrows and hardships of the past, and wine was drunk with blessings of praise and thanksgiving to God.

A three-dimensional feast, Passover celebrated the past, present and future of Israel. Passover was celebrated in order to *remember* those events of the *past* that had made Israel a people, God's people. In Hebrew the verb "to remember" is *zakar*. *Zakar* means to *make present once again*. Therefore, Passover was celebrated in order to remember, i.e., to make present once again the experiences of deliverance, of freedom, of God's special care and personal concern for Israel. During the communal sharing at the Passover meal, the Israelites also celebrated their *present* blessings, while they anticipated the joys of the *future* messianic feast.

When Jesus celebrated that last Passover with his disciples, he acted as the head of the family whose role it was to bless the food and wine and to preside over the sacred rituals. Taking the preliminary cup of wine or the *qiddush* (blessing) cup (see Luke 22:17), Jesus sanctified the day and the meal. Within the course of the meal, when it was customary for the head of the family to bless the *matzoth* or unleavened bread and to say, "This is the bread of affliction which our fathers ate as they came out of Egypt" (Exodus 16:3), Jesus took the bread and reinterpreted it in terms of himself and his imminent death: *"This is my body, which will be given for you."* No longer was it the unleavened bread which reminded Israel of past afflictions. By virtue of Jesus' words and actions, the bread he took and blessed and broke and gave to his disciples became the saving bread of his own body, which would soon be broken, in suffering and in death, in order to effect the ultimate Passover, from slavery to freedom, from sin to forgiveness, from death to life for all peoples.

The soteriological or saving character of Jesus' actions is even more pronounced in his words over the cup of blessing, which concluded the Passover meal: *"This cup is the new covenant in my blood, which will be poured out for you."* The Passover meal's cup of blessing recalled the sacrifice which sealed the Sinai covenant (Exodus 24:3-8). Moses sprinkled the blood of 12 oxen on the altar and on the people, thus confirming the relationship between Yahweh and Israel. Jesus reinterpreted the cup of blessing; he identified it with his own blood, which would soon be poured out to make a *new* covenant, a new and eternal relationship with God made possible by the atoning death of Jesus.

Early believers in Jesus recognized that his gift of himself at that Last Supper-Passover meal fulfilled the prophecy of Jeremiah,

> . . . I will make a new covenant with the House
> of Israel, but not a covenant like the one I made
> with their ancestors on the day I took them by the
> hand to lead them out of the land of Egypt. They
> broke that covenant of mine. This is the covenant
> I will make . . . I will be their God and they shall
> be my people. All shall know me from the least to
> the greatest since I will forgive their iniquity and
> never call their sin to mind. (Jeremiah 31:31-34)

This new covenant, with its forgiveness and healing, was made possible by Jesus' redeeming death. By giving his disciples the bread and wine as his body and his blood, Jesus enabled them to share in the power of his death, which brought about a new Passover and which forged a new covenant.

The triple-dimensional character (past, present, future) of the Passover feast was also evident at the Last Supper, just as it is at every Eucharistic celebration in memory of Jesus. By sharing the bread and wine which he identified as his body and blood, Jesus' disciples, then and now, *remember* him, his words, his works, his sacrificial and redeeming death, and his glorious resurrection. By sharing in the sacred meal of his body and blood, Jesus' disciples also celebrate their *present* communion with him, and anticipate the *future* heavenly banquet with him and with God in eternity.

> **THE PERFECT ASSIMILATION OF JESUS' MIND AND HEART IS NEVER A PREREQUISITE FOR CELEBRATING THE EUCHARIST.**

Immediately after Jesus had blessed his disciples with the gift of himself, Luke's gospel records a series of disappointing events: Jesus spoke of his betrayal by one of those still at table with him (Luke 22:21-23); the disciples began to argue among themselves as to whom should be regarded as the greatest among them (Luke 22:24); Peter's denials of Jesus were foretold (Luke 22:31-34); the disciples who had still not understood his mission fell asleep, leaving Jesus to pray and suffer alone in the garden (Luke 22:39-46). There is a lesson to learn in this sad turn of events. Betrayal, ambitious self-seeking, denial and misunderstanding were present in the hearts and minds of those with whom Jesus had shared that last sacred meal. But as Tad Guzie, S.J., has pointed out, "The perfect assimilation of Jesus' mentality was never a precondition of their celebrating with him." The Last Supper was not the summit, but it was itself a point in the developing relationship between Jesus and his followers. As such, it challenged those who shared it to become better, holier, more like the One by whom they had been called.

> AT EACH EUCHARIST
> WE SUBMIT OUR
> SINFULNESS TO BE
> REDEEMED AS WE
> CELEBRATE OUR
> GROWING UNION
> WITH CHRIST JESUS.

At each Eucharistic celebration, we who assemble to share the body and blood of Jesus are similarly challenged: to acknowledge the weakness, betrayal, denial, self-seeking, and lack of understanding with which we have met God and one another, and to submit these to the redeeming power of Jesus' body and blood. In that way, the sacred Eucharistic meal becomes the *confirmation* of, as well as the *means* to, and the *expression* of our union with Jesus and with one another.

Reflections

1. How was the Last Supper-Passover meal both a culmination and a commencement?

2. Explain how the feast of Passover and the gift of the Eucharist are three-dimensional events.

Chapter Six

Emmaus: A Eucharistic Encounter with the Risen Lord

According to the Lucan account of the good news, Emmaus was a village approximately seven miles from Jerusalem. As the two disciples journeyed away from Jerusalem, their spirits were downcast. They had hoped that Jesus, the great teacher and prophet from Nazareth, was the one in whom all their messianic expectations would be realized. But he had been arrested, tortured and after a trial of sorts, he had been subjected to the most heinous form of Roman execution, crucifixion. They had hoped he would have been the one to set Israel free, but now he was gone.

Those of us who enjoy the privilege of perspective, which time affords, tend to lose sight of the fact that the above scenario characterized virtually all of Jesus' followers in the period between his death and their encounters with him as risen. Because we are the fortunate heirs of an almost 2,000-year-old heritage of shared faith, we may not fully appreciate the wondrousness of the Emmaus event (Luke 24:13-35).

Jesus' disciples did *not* expect to see him again. Even when some women reported that they had found Jesus' tomb empty, they did not know how to interpret it. When he met the disciples on their way to Emmaus, they did not recognize that it was Jesus. Through the dialogue between the risen Jesus and his disciples on their way to

Emmaus, Luke illustrated for his community, and for ours, how the early believers came to faith in Jesus and in his abiding presence.

A dramatic and poignant account, the Emmaus encounter is a treasure of theological and christological insights. At the very core of the narrative, we find the authentic faith-experience of the Lucan community who, by the time the gospel was written in the 80s C.E., had taken to heart Jesus' words, "Do this as a memorial of me" (Luke 22:19). For almost two generations, they had been remembering Jesus at their shared meals. At one point in their meal, they took bread, blessed it, broke it and gave it to one another, realizing that as they did so they were remembering Jesus' death and all that he had said and done; they were celebrating their present communion with him and they were anticipating their future joy with God in eternity. The Emmaus narrative serves to bring out more fully the significance of the Last Supper-Eucharistic event, viz., that their sacred Eucharistic sharing was not only the *means* by which the disciples would *remember* Jesus . . . it would also be the *means* by which they would *continue* to *experience his presence.*

What happened on the way to Emmaus was an event that continues to teach, encourage and edify all who believe in Jesus.

The fact that the disciples did not immediately recognize Jesus (Luke 24:16) indicates that he was somehow different; in his risen state he was transformed. Still unrecog-

> AT EACH EUCHARIST, THE PRESENCE OF JESUS IS REMEMBERED, EXPERIENCED AND CELEBRATED.

nized, Jesus took the scriptures and explained to them all those passages that should have prepared them for understanding his mission and purpose.

In the period after Jesus' resurrection, the early Christians continued to draw on the Old Testament. Texts such as the Emmanuel prophecies of Isaiah (7:14-16; 9:1-7; 11:1-9), the Suffering Servant Songs of Deutero-Isaiah (42:1-4; 49:1-6; 50:4-11; 52:13-53:12), and the Psalms (22, 35, 118, etc.) were helpful in explaining to those who rejected the idea of a suffering, dying Messiah that Jesus' ministry, and even his suffering and death, had been part of God's saving plan for humankind.

> When their eyes were opened, the disciples recognized the continuity between the Last Supper, the Cross and the Risen Jesus.

After this instruction, the still unrecognized Jesus appeared ready to part company with the two disciples, but they pressed him, "Stay with us!" And as the narrative continues, Jesus goes on to show them the means by which he actually would *stay* with his disciples . . . *He took the bread and blessed it and broke it and gave it to them* . . . At that moment, the disciples' eyes were opened; they recognized Jesus as risen and alive! They became aware of the continuity between the risen Jesus at Emmaus and the Jesus who had taken and blessed and broken bread to give to the crowds (Luke 9:10-17), as well as the Jesus of the Last Supper who took, blessed, broke and gave the bread as his own Body. The Emmaus experience illustrated the fact that the table communion and meal sharing that was interrupted by the death of Jesus was resumed by the risen Christ.

Notably, the narrative follows a pattern similar to our contemporary Eucharistic liturgies, wherein the believing community encounters Jesus in both Word and Sacrament. At Emmaus, the risen Christ first broke the "bread" of the Scriptures to nourish and enlighten the disciples; today, at every Eucharistic celebration, we are first nourished and enlightened through the Liturgy of the Word. Then, just as the risen Jesus at Emmaus was recognized as he *took* and *blessed* and *broke* and *gave* the bread which he identified as his Body, so too, at every Eucharistic celebration, the community which is nourished by the Body of Christ continues to recognize and to experience his abiding presence. In the breaking of the Bread of his Word and of his Body, Jesus remains with the community, which professes him as Lord.

Jesus' contemporaries, with their rich traditions of the Passover feast and of shared meals, were well-prepared for understanding the gift of himself and of his continued presence in the sacred sharing of the Eucharist. The early Christians continued the tradition of the shared meal, and within that context remembered and repeated Jesus' actions at the Last Supper. Both events, the shared meal and the Lord's Supper or Eucharist helped to define and celebrate the other. The shared meal, with its opportunity for communal sharing, love and mutual giving, aided in their understanding of the Eucharist as the ultimate source of their union. The Eucharistic celebration, in turn, gave meaning and expression to every aspect of the life of the community.

But by the early third century C.E., and for a variety
of reasons, including those cited by Paul in his letter to
the Church at Corinth (1 Corinthians 11:17-34), the meal
setting of the Eucharist had completely disappeared. During the reign of Constantine in the fourth century, the
house churches were replaced by church buildings, erected
specifically for worship. With the disappearance of the
house churches, common meals were less prevalent, and
the rich tradition which had provided the Eucharist with
its original context was no longer present. Gradually, the
liturgy became more and more elaborate, and congrega-
tional participation declined. Not until Vatican II, and the
renewal which it initiated, was the Eucharistic liturgy restored to its original purpose and structure. Still, it is difficult to inculcate the character of the Eucharist as a shared
meal, wherein Jesus' saving death is remembered, and
wherein he becomes present, when so many in our modern culture have so little experience of the richness of the
shared meal.

In his encyclical *Evangelii Nuntiandi*, Pope Paul VI
underscored the continuing need for pre-evangelization.
Before the gospel of Jesus Christ can be preached (evan-
gelization) and before faith in Jesus can be shared
(catechesis), the basic human groundwork must be established (pre-evangelization). For understanding the good
news about the Eucharist, the basic human groundwork of
shared meals, mutual care and loving support should be
established within the family unit. These elements provide
a fitting matrix for a growing faith in the Eucharist as the
source and center of our life in Christ. Traditions and
celebrations that create and confirm the family also create
the basis and impetus for future families. Just as Jesus
made every shared meal an opportunity for knowing and
experiencing the saving love and forgiveness of God, so

should our shared meals be "teachable moments," wherein Christian values and faith may develop and growing believers may attain authentic maturity in Christ.

Within this framework, we shall be more fittingly prepared to recognize and receive the Lord Jesus when he makes himself known to us in the Breaking of the Bread.

Reflections

1. How do contemporary liturgies resemble the Emmaus encounter?

2. What factors contributed to the loss of the meal setting for the Eucharist?

3. How could this loss be remedied?

Prophecy

CHAPTER ONE

Origin and Development

Whenever someone mentions the terms "prophet" or "prophecy" today, many of us conjure up one of two images. Some of us may recall that select group of individuals whose missions were exercised in the ancient near east over 2,500 years ago. Others of us are prompted to think of those modern-day, street-corner or door-to-door heralds, who claim to know the future and whose unpopular message of warning and doom is communicated to disinterested passersby via pamphlets, fliers or placards.

The phenomenon of prophecy in its truest sense is an integral part of our past tradition *and* a viable, formative aspect of our present reality. Just as we may not relegate the gift of prophecy to the distant past, we may not overlook its valid and authoritative presence in contemporary society.

In Hebrew, there were several words which pertained to the ministry of the prophet. *Hozeh* or "visionary" designated the manner in which the prophets received their messages. *Ro'eh* or "seer" (1 Samuel 9), another name for the prophet, referred to that special insight whereby the prophet could perceive what others could not. "Man of God" was a title which referred

> **The prophet functions as God's mouthpiece in society.**

169

to the prophet's God-given access to divine power, a power which enabled the prophet to heal, to bring to life, etc. (1 Kings 17 – 2 Kings 10). Most common among the Hebrew names for the prophet was the term *nabi*, meaning "one who is called by God." As God's *nabi* or prophet, the one who was called by God served as a legitimate and authoritative link between God and humankind. The English word, prophet, is derived from the Greek word, *prophetes*, which literally means mouthpiece. More than the other designations, *prophetes* or mouthpiece underscored the fact that the prophet spoke, *not his own*, or *her own*, but *God's word*. As God's living and active word, the prophetic message, once uttered, has a life of its own; it continues to speak and must not be censured or ignored. Greater than the prophet whose burden it was to deliver, the word of God is eternally valid and timely, applicable to every people of every age.

At its earliest stages of development, the phenomenon of prophecy was manifested quite simply among the Israelites. But this phenomenon was not restricted to Israel or uniquely Jewish. In fact, anthropological studies have shown that prophecy and prophets can arise spontaneously in any society in which the necessary social and religious conditions are present.

Studies of ancient Babylonian and Assyrian records have shown that from a very early period (18th B.C.E.) prophets or seers were a recognized part of the religious hierarchy. By reading or divining the will of the gods through unusual signs in natural objects, prophets were thought to be able to mediate that will to humankind. For example, pagan prophets observed the movements of the stars or the flight of a flock of birds and concluded therefrom a divine message. So too, the entrails of animals and/or the cross-sectioned liver of a sheep were thought to contain a sacred communiqué.

In ancient Israel such methods of divination were regarded as pagan superstitions and were forbidden. Still, there is evidence that Israel's first prophets made use of the *urim* and *thummim* (an instrument for casting of lots) as a means of asking God for a "yes" or "no" answer (1 Samuel 14:18, 36-37, 41; 23:10-13).

Israel's earliest prophets sometimes accepted remuneration for their favors. For example, when consulted about a lost animal, or about the tides of war, prophets were duly paid for their services. These earliest prophets, sometimes referred to as "guilds of" or "sons of prophets," often lived together on the outskirts of the village or city. At times, these groups engaged in frenzied singing or dancing, which pro-

> CHAMPIONS of THE POOR, THE PROPHETS GAVE VOICE TO THOSE WHO HAD BEEN SILENCED.

duced a trance-like or ecstatic state. Some of these prophets were on the temple or royal payroll and were consulted for favors or messages as situations arose. By the late ninth and early eighth century, these prophetic guilds and their primitive style of prophesying had yielded to the more developed methods of the writing or classical prophets.

Whereas the primitive prophets had been concerned with discerning God's will for specific individuals, these later prophets spoke to the entire nation of Israel. Through their oracles, both oral and written, the eighth-century (and thereafter) prophets challenged what they perceived as the false values of their contemporaries, while reminding their people of the basic principles which were to regulate and guide their lives, e.g., the covenant, monotheism, etc.

Champions of the poor, these later prophets gave voice to those who had been silenced and spoke out for society's victims, for the poor, the underprivileged, etc. Because they were usually not affiliated with any particular human power-base, the prophets were free to criticize and to chastise royalty and clergy, as well as the ordinary common folk. Contributing a valuable and powerful new factor to Israel's growing awareness of itself as a people, the writing or classical prophets made their contemporaries *ethically* aware of themselves and their responsibilities. In other words, the prophets functioned as a social conscience, raising unpopular questions and confronting popular, but unexamined values, with God's own word. Sentinels of society, and guardians of God's truth, the prophets have not been silenced, nor has their message lost its relevance. For all who believe, the prophets' insights remain a constant challenge.

Reflections

1. Do you believe that prophets still exist?
2. Is there a need for them in our society? Why?

Chapter Two

The Three R's of Prophetic Vocation

Very little biographical or autobiographical material has been included in the prophetic books of the Bible. Concerned more with their message than with themselves as its mediator, the prophets chose to leave unanswered many questions with regard to their backgrounds and personal lives. A few of the prophets, however, have shared with their readers the *general* circumstances concerning their prophetic vocations. Because of this sharing, the prophets have given to all believers a general model by which to understand the different aspects or stages of Christian vocation. A simple way to recall these successive steps is to call them the "Three R's" of Prophetic Vocation.

The first "*R*" stands for *RECOGNITION*. At the very outset, the one called by God for service had to recognize and evaluate the genuineness and/or authenticity of the call. At times, the help of another was needed. For example, the young Samuel was helped by Eli to recognize that it was God who was calling him (1 Samuel 3). When he was called by God, the Prophet Isaiah (Isaiah 6) had been at work at the temple. Because of this fact, it is generally believed that Isaiah was a cultic prophet. Since he was in the Holy of Holies, the most sacred part of the temple sanctuary, where only the high priest entered once a year on the feast of Yom Kippur (Day of Atonement), we may also assume that Isaiah was a priest (and, for that year, *high priest*). At the very moment when Isaiah recognized that his was a genuine encounter with God, Isaiah became painfully aware of himself as a sinful person. Like all who encounter the great God of goodness and holiness, Isaiah drew back, overwhelmed by his own unworthiness. "*Oy Veh!*", he cried. "Woe is me! I'm a sinner and I belong to a sinful people!"

Thus the second "*R*" could be described as *RETICENCE* or *REPENTANCE*. When Jeremiah was called, he thought of himself as unequal to the task because of his age; he was reticent and begged God to find someone else (Jeremiah 1:6-7). Jonah, the protagonist in the Bible's greatest fish story, was reluctant and even rebellious when called by God. Jonah didn't necessarily doubt his own capabilities, but he was repulsed by the thought of bringing God's word to a people he hated, the Ninevites (Jonah 1:1-2). Legend has it that Habakkuk was so reticent at the thought of being God's spokesperson that he had to be carried by the hair of his head to his appointed duties! Normal human reactions, the reticence or repentance exhibited by the prophets were transformed by God's power and grace into a spirit of willingness and eagerness to serve.

This final stage in the process of vocation could be labeled with a third "*R*" for *READINESS*. Samuel, once he had been counseled by Eli, responded readily to God's call, "Here I am, Lord." When Isaiah understood that it would be through *God's power* and in God's name

To RECOGNIZE AN AUTHENTIC CALL FROM God REQUIRES PRAYER, COUNSEL AND CONTINUAL REEVALUATION.

that he would speak, the prophet eagerly volunteered, "Here I am, send me" (Isaiah 6:9). Even Jeremiah, who often lamented bitterly at the thought of bearing God's word to an unwilling audience . . . "I am a daily laughing-stock . . . the word of Yahweh has meant for me insult, derision, all day long" (Jeremiah 20:7-8) . . . even Jeremiah acquiesced to God's power and preached the word which could "tear up and knock down, destroy and overthrow, build and plant" (Jeremiah 1:10).

When considering the various stages and/or attitudes which have been and are still a part of our *own* vocations to come to know God and to serve one another, we will probably be able to distinguish each of the three "*R*'s." *R*ecognition of a call, as true and as authentic, requires prayer, counsel and continual *re*-evaluation. God does not call us only *once*; rather God extends many invitations and challenges to us on many occasions through different people and within the changing circumstances of our lives. In a given lifetime, God, in patient mercy, renews issues several calls, giving new direction and scope to our vocation. The same God who guided Isaiah, Samuel, Amos, et al., is always present, inspiring believers to write our own chapters in the ever-developing story of our salvation.

At times the burden of our inadequacies, the discouragement over our failures or the seeming insurmountableness of the task at hand may cause us to be *ret*icent or even to *reb*el. When God calls us in these instances, it is

> God's GRACE ANd CREATiVE POWER CAN lifT US AbOVE OUR WEAkNESSES ANd PROMPT US TO GREAT THiNGS.

necessary to allow God's grace and creative power to lift us above our weakness and to enable us to be and to do great things for God and others.

We have only to look to the lives of the prophets to find solace and encouragement. Not one of them could boast of a Ph.D. or even a master's degree in theology. Amos was a migrant worker who tended both sheep and sycamore trees as the seasons dictated. He had no impressive résumé to flaunt when he confronted the high priest, Amaziah (Amos 7:10ff). All Amos had, all *any* of the prophets had, was the word of God and the charge to speak that word in truth and in faith.

In each of the prophets, even in the griping Jeremiah, the bigoted Jonah and the frightened Habakkuk, modern believers can find a model of Readiness to admire and to imitate. In their willingness to rely on the power of God and the message of truth, the prophets remain an inspiration to us. Their worlds and the people to whom they bore God's word were no more or less difficult than our own. Because we rely on God's grace to enhance our own personal and God-given talents, each of us can echo the response of Samuel and Isaiah:

Here I am, Lord. Send me!

Reflections

1. What are the "three R's" of prophetic vocation?
2. Can you discern these three R's in your own life?

Chapter Three

Prophets As Social Conscience

It is doubtful that Amos or the other prophets received many invitations to parties or other social gatherings. After all, who would enjoy the company of a guest whose very presence threatened to dampen the gracious ambiance which the host had labored to establish? Who would care or even dare to chitchat with one whose insults and observations made it difficult to digest the hors d'oeuvres? In one of his more colorful repartees, the prophet Amos had this to say about the party-goers of Israel:

> Listen to this word, you cows, who oppress the needy and crush the poor, saying to your husbands, "Bring us something to drink!" . . . You lie in your ivory beds and sprawl on your sofas, dining on lambs and stall-fattened veal. You drink wine by the bowlful and use the finest perfumes . . . I will destroy both your winter and summer homes, says the Lord, I will punish you for all your crimes against the poor! (Amos 4:1, 6:4-6, 3:15).

What made the prophets of Israel such party-poopers?

What made Amos and his prophetic colleagues such "party-poopers"? Why couldn't they just sit back and ensconce themselves in the lap of luxury, like so many of

177

their contemporaries? It was true that during the eighth century B.C.E., and during the prophetic careers of Isaiah, Hosea, Amos and Micah, Israel had reached a political peak; some have called it her "golden age." But the wealth of the nation was enjoyed only by a pampered few, and oppression of the lower classes was rife. Most of the well-to-do people attributed their prosperity to God's blessings, lavished on the people chosen to be God's very own. Believing themselves to be God's special elect, and above all other peoples, the Israelites fell prey to a condition which we might call "chosen-people-itis."

This condition resulted from a misinterpretation of the covenant relationship which Israel enjoyed with Yahweh. Some had chosen to concentrate only on the blessings and privileges of the covenant and, subsequently, had overlooked the duties and responsibilities inherent in their special relationship with God. In reminding his people of the fact that their calling bore *special* responsibilities, Amos admonished, "You *only* have I known of all the families of the earth; *therefore* I will punish you for all your iniquities." (Amos 3:2)

> As champions of God's justice, the prophets shattered the complacent torpor of their people and reawakened them to their responsibilities.

Among Israel's special responsibilities was the challenge to "be holy as the Lord your God is Holy" (Leviticus 17-26), and to "hate evil, love good and establish justice in the gate" (Amos 5:15). The holiness and justice to which all of God's elect were called demanded of the community a quality of life wherein the needs of *each* and every person was met. True justice protected the rights of all individuals and was to reflect the generous manner with which God had dealt with humankind throughout history. Justice, i.e., the justice of the covenanting God, aimed not only at *enforcing* the law, but of *restoring* its integrity in every instance where the absence of God's law had resulted in human suffering. As champions of God's justice, the prophets set out to shatter the complacent torpor of their people and to reawaken them to their responsibilities. For this reason the prophets took upon themselves the role of being the reflective *social conscience* of their people.

Significantly the term "conscience," as the autonomous guide of an individual, was not known in the Hebrew Scriptures. Human conscience, as we know it today, was not preached by the prophets, nor was it the basis of the moral behavior to which they called their people. Rather, *God's own will*, as revealed through the law and articulated by the prophets, was to be the starting point of all ethical behavior. Religion and ethics were bound in Israel by a strongly developed *consciousness* that the foundations of all moral law and therefore of ethical behavior rested in the Lord. "It is God who knows what is good," taught the author of Proverbs (3:5), and Micah reminded, "What is good has been explained to you, my people!" (6:8). The Deuteronomist enjoined his people to learn and to understand God's will, "Let these words be written on your heart . . . repeat them to your children . . . write them on your door frames and on your gates" (Deuteronomy 6:6-9). By knowing and assimilating the divine will and loving ways, Israel was then able to live morally and to respond with integrity to God.

In Judaism and Christianity, as well as in the other major religions of the world, the relationship between persons is fundamentally determined by the relationship which exists between God and the individual. Continually the prophets reminded the Israelites of this fact. No one could claim to have a true relationship with God unless the truth of that relationship were reflected in loving, caring interaction with other human beings. If the vertical (between God and the individual) and horizontal (between individuals) dimensions of the covenantal relationship are not bound together in a balanced tension, then both of the so-called relationships are a lie and a sham. But when proper relational balance is maintained in a holy and wholesome society, then the poor are cared for, the hungry are fed, the naked are clothed and the sick are no longer lonely and afraid. When the will of God truly forms and guides the human conscience, then wars will cease and military weaponry will be relegated to the museum or the scrap heap. When the prophetic voice of social consciousness is able to resonate in kindred hearts, then there will be no more travesties of justice, such as now exist in Sudan, Rwanda, Bosnia, the former Soviet bloc and, yes, even in the U.S. When God's holiness and justice is translated into human activity, and when God's ways are allowed to fully inform human values, then Amos and others like him, will no longer be unwelcome party guests.

Reflections

1. What does it mean to be a social conscience?
2. In the Hebrew Scriptures, what is the basis of the human conscience?

Chapter Four

The Prophets and Religion

Imagine, if you will, the following scenario: Someone, not very appropriately attired for the occasion, enters the cathedral during the Sunday Eucharistic Celebration. The Archbishop in full regalia is concelebrating with several other priests. With vibrant, if not completely harmonious voices, the choir responds to the cantor's lead. Incense fills the air. Adults listen patiently, punctuating their silent attentiveness with an occasional cough or sneeze; children fidget and flip through the pages of the hymnals. Suddenly the poorly dressed visitor stands up in the center aisle and shouts aloud for all to hear:

> This is what God has to say about your liturgy . . . "I hate and despise your feasts, I take no pleasure in your solemn festivals . . . Let me have no more of the din of your chanting, no more of your strumming on harps . . . Bring me your worthless offerings no more, I cannot endure your solemnities. When you multiply your prayers, I shall not listen" (Amos 5:21-27; Isaiah 1:12-17).

While the congregation sits in shock, considering whether or not the visitor is mad or just a misguided religious fanatic, one of the assembly rises and counters, "Then with what gifts shall we come to the Lord?" (Micah 6:6). Quietly and deliberately the visitor responds,

What is good has already been explained to you . . .
this is what God asks of you . . . only this: to act
justly, to love tenderly and to walk humbly with your
God . . . what I want from you, my people is love,
not sacrifice, knowledge of God, not holocausts!" (Micah 6:7-8, Hosea 6:6).

If your imagination has served you well, the preced-
ing narrative may have left you with the same sense of
shock and outrage experienced by those who heard the
prophets. But this was precisely the intention of the
prophets, i.e., to disrupt the *status quo*, to shake into
awareness those for whom religion and liturgy had become a routine and thoughtless exercise.

> IT WAS THE INTENTION OF THE PROPHETS TO DISRUPT THE STATUS QUO AND TO SHAKE INTO AWARENESS THOSE FOR WHOM RELIGION AND LITURGY HAD BECOME A ROUTINE AND THOUGHTLESS EXERCISES.

Because of their strongly expressed views about Israel's cult, a few biblical scholars have asserted that pre-exilic (before 587 B.C.E.) prophets were entirely opposed to Israel's practice of animal sacrifice as a *less worthy* manner of worshipping Yahweh. These scholars have suggested that animal sacrifice was a Canaanite import and embodied an inferior idea of religion. In fact, however, the prophets were not opposed to the cult or liturgy of sacrifice, per se, but to the *manner* and/or *motivation* which inspired these rituals. When the external acts of animal sacrifice, or the offering of incense, or even choral singing and public prayer were not matched by a sincere interior disposition and then translated into a life of loving service and personal integrity, the prophets cried, "Hypocrisy!" and called for reform. As Bruce Vawter, an eminent Scripture scholar and expert on the prophets has observed, "The prophets were not concerned with the issue of external forms of worship as an ideal or abstraction." What was at issue, then, in the eighth century B.C.E., and is still at issue now in the 20th century C.E., are the acts of worship being carried out in sanctuaries by those who perpetrate a sacramentalism devoid of meaning. Perhaps a contemporary mode of expressing the prophetic ideal would be as follows: "Why come to Mass and go through the motions of celebrating the Lord's presence when your actions during the rest of the day and for the remainder of the week are not consonant with your Sunday experience?!"

Besides criticizing the oftentimes empty and hypocritical liturgies of their contemporaries, the prophets were also a major force in establishing a strictly monotheistic religion in Israel. When Israel's attention strayed and when the people were enamored of the pantheon of gods of which the other nations boasted, it was the prophets who called them back to the one, true God, who was above all others.

> DEPENDING UPON THE CIRCUMSTANCES, THE PROPHETS WERE MINISTERS OF CHASTISEMENT AND/OR COMFORT FOR THEIR PEOPLE.

Hosea had a particularly unique method of calling his people back to God. Using his own unhappy marital experiences as a vehicle for his message (Hosea 1-3), Hosea compared Israel to his own wife, Gomer. Though she had been a known prostitute, Hosea married Gomer, began a family with her, and when she regressed to her former ways, Hosea sought her out, lovingly forgave her and took her back into his home. Comparing Israel's idolatry to his wife's adultery, Hosea called the people to turn away from their idols and to return to the one God, who would forgive them and continue to love them, despite their infidelities. While Hosea's theology understood that Yahweh was superior to other gods, it still admitted that other gods, however inferior, existed. Not until the sixth century B.C.E., and with the uncompromising monotheism reflected by Deutero-Isaiah, did Israel fully understand that Yahweh was not only above all other gods, but that there *were no other gods!* (Isaiah 44:6-8, 45:4-6,20-22).

A third major contribution of the prophets toward the religious development of Judaism was their messianic theology. When the monarchy failed to reflect God's holiness and justice among the people, the prophets preached of a future leader who would accomplish God's purposes (2 Samuel 7:14, Isaiah 7:14-17, 9:1-7, 11:1-9).

Keeping alive the hopes of their people, even during the desperate years of their exile in Babylonia, the prophets assured Israel that their messiah, i.e., their saving Lord, would intervene on their behalf (Isaiah 40:1-5, 10-11). When Israel's expectations became too political and nationalistic, the prophets tried to reshape and broaden their hopes. Deutero-Isaiah's servant-savior (Isaiah 42:1-9, 49:1-6, 50:4-9, 52:13-53:12) was portrayed as one who would bring *all peoples* to the light of salvation by his innocent, vicarious sufferings.

Christians owe a great debt to the prophets of Israel, because their insights into God's ways and their fidelity to God's word have helped us to understand:

(1) the mystery of Jesus' saving passion and death as part of the divine plan of salvation;

(2) the oneness and uniqueness of God;

(3) the necessity of integrity and authenticity in worship.

For this reason, the prophets must continue to be read and heeded as relevant voices of God's truth in our world.

Reflections

1. What were three of the major contributions of the prophets?

2. How did messianic hope emerge and develop in Israel?

Chapter Five

Prophets in the Christian Era

Although believers in Jesus and the authors of the Christian Scriptures understood otherwise, the Jewish rabbis of the first century C.E. taught their followers that God had ceased to speak to humankind through the medium of prophecy. With the fall of Jerusalem and the Babylonian exile, prophecy, a centuries-old institution, underwent radical changes. Since the monarchy had been dissolved, it made little sense to speak of the blessings that God would shower on the people through the king. Nor could the prophets validly admonish the people and threaten the loss of their kingdom if they did not repent. However, as Lawrence Boadt has observed in his excellent text, *Reading the Old Testament* (Paulist Press: 1984), the prophets from Jeremiah to Zechariah were confronted with new situations, never before dealt with by their predecessors; therefore they responded with new solutions. The resultant shift in the nature and scope of prophecy was geared toward matters of daily living and worship. Since Israel was no longer free to make autonomous political decisions (after

> WHEN THE PROPHETS WERE CONFRONTED WITH NEW SITUATIONS, THEY RESPONDED WITH NEW SOLUTIONS.

the Babylonian conquerors came the Persians, the Syrians, the Greeks and the Romans), prophecy lost its effectiveness with regard to political matters, and subsequently directed its attention to the rebuilding of community life *for the future.*

Of course, the prophets continued to uphold their commitment to social justice and covenantal fidelity, but in focusing on a new and different approach to God, the prophets gradually put themselves out of business. Formerly, prophetism had flourished in the tension between power politics and loyalty to Yahweh. But as Boadt explained, "when only the area of worship was left to Israel's decision-making, prophecy gradually disappeared and was replaced by one of two options: by *priestly instruction* (the way of the Torah), or by a visionary hope for the future expressed in apocalyptic forms.

Such was the situation in Judaism in the first Christian century. But with the appearance of Jesus, as God's ultimate message to humankind, and with the recognition of Jesus as Lord and Savior, it became obvious that prophecy had *not* ceased. On the contrary, Christians believe that all prophecy concerning salvation has been fulfilled by the person and through the mission of Jesus. For this reason, Léon-Dufour has described the New Testament (or the Christian scriptures) as the con-

> With the appearance of Jesus, it became clear that prophecy had not been eliminated but had come to full flower.

scious fulfillment of the prophecies of the Old Testament (or Hebrew Scriptures). With the appearance of Jesus, it became clear that prophecy had not been eliminated but had come to full flower. All that the Old Testament prophets had foretold concerning the messianic age (e.g., Joel 3:1, Isaiah 61, etc.) had become a reality in and through Jesus. During his ministry, many recognized and acclaimed Jesus, not merely as *one* of the prophets but as *The Prophet*, like Moses (Matthew 16:14, Luke 7:16, John 4:19, 9:17). According to the Deuteronomist, God had promised that he would raise up for his people a prophet who would speak in God's name and bring life to his people (Deuteronomy 18:9-22).

Apart from Jesus himself, John the Baptizer was one of the preeminent Christian prophets. Each of the evangelists recognized John as the herald of a new age. Straddling both testaments, the Baptizer drew together the testimony of his ancestors and directed it toward Jesus. "All the prophets as well as the Law have prophesied to the time of John," wrote Matthew (11:13) and Luke (16:16). In other words, all of Jewish prophecy came to a climax in John's ministry as he directed all his followers to see Jesus as the fulfiller of all prophecies.

In addition to John the Baptizer, there were other New Testament personalities who exercised the prophetic ministry. Recall Simeon, through whom God revealed the universal scope of Jesus' saving mission (Luke 2:29-32). Remember also the prophetess, Anna, who recognized Jesus as Messiah and joyfully spread the good news of his appearance to all whom she met (Luke 2:36-38). In the New Testament, just as in the Jewish tradition, the ministry of prophetism was shared by both men and women, with no distinction as to the importance or effectiveness of their role (Exodus 15:20-21, 2 Kings 22:14-20, Nehemiah 6:10-14, Revelation 2:20).

After Jesus' death and resurrection, prophecy and prophets continued to play a very important role in the development of the early church. Significantly, the outpouring of the Spirit, which Luke has portrayed as taking place on the feast of Pentecost (Acts 2:14-21), resulted in a powerful manifestation of the prophetic charism. Considered to be a gift of the Holy Spirit, prophecy helped the first believers in Jesus to interpret his life and his teachings in the light of ancient Testament prophecies (Matthew 13:57, 21:11; Luke 4:24).

Some of the Christian communities integrated prophecy into their worship services (1 Thessalonians 5:20, 1 Corinthians 12:28-29, 14:26-32). In the second volume of his two-volume work, Luke tells us that the church in Antioch had both prophets and teachers to conduct the liturgy (Acts 13:2). This practice was echoed in the Didache (10:7), wherein the Christian prophets were said to preside at the Eucharist. According to Raymond E. Brown, "Association of the prophet with the eucharist is not so strange, when we realize that the New Testament prophets, men and women, were concerned with the future, and the eucharist was thought to proclaim 'the Lord's death until he comes'" (1 Corinthians 11:26).

At an early date, prophesying became the province of a specialized office in the church, and prophets were ranked with apostles and teachers as church leaders (Acts 11:27, 13:1, 15:32; Ephesians 2:20, 3:5, 4:11; James 5:10; 1 Peter 1:10; Revelation 22:6-9). Because the danger of *false* prophecy also carried over into New Testament times, it was necessary for the community, guided by the Holy Spirit, to discern the true from the false prophets. In the Didache it was suggested that prophets who remained in one place for an extended period of time, and who thereby became an economic burden to the community, were very likely false prophets. So too were those who, while purporting to speak in prophetic ecstasy, ordered a meal or demanded money! (Didache XI 712, XII-XIII).

What then would be the criteria for recognizing the true prophet? Paul recommended that the validity of prophecy could be judged in the measure that the prophet built up, exhorted and consoled the community for the benefit of the common good (1 Corinthians 14:3, 29-32).

Reflections

1. How did the prophetic ministry evolve after the Babylonian exile?

2. What are the criteria by which a true prophet can be identified?

CHAPTER SIX

WHERE HAVE ALL THE PROPHETS GONE?

Some day, said Paul when writing to the church at Corinth, "prophecy will cease" (1 Corinthians 13:8). Indeed, there *will* come a time, at the end of time, when prophesying will no longer be necessary because "we shall see God face to face" (1 Corinthians 13:12) and have no further need of intermediaries. But *until* that time, advised Paul in the same letter, we should "set our hearts on spiritual gifts . . . above all the gift of prophecy . . . the prophet speaks to the community for its building up, encouragement and consolation . . . the one who prophesies builds up the church" (1 Corinthians 14:2-4). Prophecy did not cease with the death of Zechariah or Malachi; nor did it die out with the apostolic age. As Xavier Léon-Dufour has pointed out, it would be difficult to understand the mission of many saints in the church without reference to the charism of prophecy. In fact, to deny the continued existence of and necessity of prophets and prophecy

> **The prophets knew that the past wasn't final nor was the present complete because God's oracle of salvation is still being sung.**

in our world would be to deny an integral aspect of the church's apostolic mission.

In both the Hebrew and Christian Scriptures, the prophets were men and women who spoke, by their words and by their lives, for God. They had been given an understanding of God's will and God's ways and, because of this insight, the biblical prophets would not allow their contemporaries to settle for anything less. Future-minded individuals, the prophets knew that the past wasn't final, nor was the present complete, for God's oracle of salvation was still being sung and had to be experienced by all peoples. For that reason, Jeremiah, Isaiah, Amos, Nahum, Micah, John the Baptizer, Anna, Huldah, etc., caused their contemporaries to critically question their lives, their world, its standards, and to discern the real meaning of God's will for God's people.

Are there not such people in the world today?

Are there not individuals who are called to a similar ministry in the community of humankind?

Obviously, the answer is a resounding YES! Whenever and wherever believers bring the truth of God's Word to bear on lived experience, to interpret it and to challenge the community to a Christian response, these believers perform a prophetic service and are truly God's prophets. Whenever people are caused to reflect critically on their lives in light of the gospel, and whenever people are moved to deal creatively, courageously and *christianly* with reality, then prophecy is happening!

Who can doubt or deny that the spirit of prophecy continues to live and to be exercised in:

• the person of Mother Teresa of Calcutta, whose attention to the pariah of the world reflects God's own compassion and concern for humankind?

- the voices of our American bishops, who speak out against nuclear proliferation and an economic system that victimizes the poor?
- the blood of the four martyred missionaries in El Salvador?
- the suffering of those Rwandan people, whose rights and dignity are denied them due to the sins of prejudice and hatred?
- the cries for justice of Archbishop Tutu, Nelson Mandela, Vaclav Havel and so many others, who have called to the rest of the world community for assistance?
- the voices of the world's children, who remind us of what it means to be innocent and guileless?

Who can doubt that the spirit of prophecy continues to live and to speak in:

- those who dare to dissent when it would be so much easier to let things ride and to bow to the "status quo"?
- those who translate their Sunday piety into honesty and charity in the work place?
- the stare of the starving child, who has no more strength to beg for food or even to cry, but waits silently for death's relief?
- the desperate need of the farmers, who have lost their land because there is no market for their crops?
- the loneliness of the aged, whose children are too busy to call or to visit?

There are, of course, a myriad of other examples of the presence of prophecy and prophets in our world. I would propose that *every* believer is called to be prophetic, i.e., to be so personally involved in God's word as

> **WE CAN'T All bE GREAT pROphETS bUT WE All CAN bE sMAll pROphETS.**

to live each hour of each day for that word and to be ultimately prepared to die for it. Thomas H. Groome, in his book *Christian Religious Education*, has said that we can't all be great prophets but can all be small prophets. As best we can, we need to urge ourselves and others to question our world and to actively guide it in the direction of the kingdom.

Naturally, says Groome, some caution must be observed in acting and living prophetically. There may be a tendency to suppose that the prophet's task is primarily a negative one, i.e., to criticize or to chastise. But true criticism must be a positive activity exercised for the sake of recreating and renewing the community. "The prophetic word is a two-edged sword which, in the midst of its mandate, brings affirmation, and in the midst of its criticism brings consolation" (T. Groome).

Finally, the prophet must always bear in mind that he/she is a member of the community, not *over* it or *above* it, but an integral part of a whole, who is nourished and complemented by the other members of the human family. No one person "has the corner of the prophetic market"; indeed, only in the midst of the community can the prophet's words be refined and enhanced. Prophets don't just speak or write or act; they must also listen, learn and share.

In conclusion, we may ask once again, "Where have all the prophets gone? Does prophecy still exist?" Inasmuch as Christians remain a viable reflection of God's truth in the world, the voice of the prophet will be heard.

Insofar as you and I continue to hear and to be faithful to God's living word in whomever and however it is spoken, prophecy will survive . . . until we see God face to face and know God fully, intimately and forever.

Reflections

1. Have you ever known a prophet personally?
2. Would you be willing to serve others as a prophet? How? Why?

Reconciliation

CHAPTER ONE

THE ROOT AND THE FLOWER OF TRUE RELIGION

One hot afternoon in mid-July 1930, the great German professor Albert Einstein invited the noted Indian scholar and mystic, Rabindranath Tagore, to his home. As the two Nobel laureates exchanged ideas on a variety of topics, the subject of their conversation eventually turned to religion. Whereas one man's spirituality was influenced by his scientific background, the other's grew from a more mystical and philosophical framework. Both, however, agreed that the heart of all religion was the personal relationship between the infinite God and finite humanity, and that the basic tenor of that relationship was characterized by a lifelong process of reconciliation.

"My religion *is* reconciliation," explained Tagore, "the reconciliation of all human spirits with one another and of all human spirits together with the Divine." But long before these two great men conversed on a hot July afternoon in Kaputh, India, the notion of reconciliation had been an essential aspect of true religion.

> RECONCILIATION IS A PROCESS OF COMING EYEBROW-TO-EYEBROW TOGETHER AGAIN IN PEACE.

Reconciliation, according to the *American Heritage Dictionary*, may be defined as the "reestablishment of a friendship" and/or the "calling together again of an assembly." The very mention of the concept of reconciliation presupposes *first* that a relationship once existed, and *second*, that some rift had occurred which damaged that relationship, thus alienating those once bound in union with one another. If the word reconciliation were broken down into its root elements, a fascinating and somewhat different perception of the concept is unearthed. The prefix "re" means "again"; the term "con" means "together." "Cilia" are tiny hairs or hairlike projectiles, like eyelashes or eye-brows. "Tion" is a suffix which means "process" or "action." Put all these elements together and reconciliation could be thought of as the process of coming eyebrow-to-eyebrow together again!

All of us are familiar with the joys and difficulties involved in the process of reconciliation between persons. One or the other person must make the first move toward the other. There is usually an admission of fault, both must agree on terms, and eventually new agreements are forged. Occasionally no agreement can be reached, and alienation persists; there is no reconciliation. It is, however, an entirely different matter when one considers the reconciliation between God and humankind.

Some have said that the entire Bible, in both the Hebrew and Christian Scriptures, bears witness to that process of reconciliation whereby sinful humanity is once again established in friendship with God. Within the first pages of Genesis, the biblical author poetically portrayed the pristine relationship which existed when God and humankind walked together in an idyl-

> RECONCILIATION is both the root and flower of authentic religion.

lic setting; their harmony was reflected in the order and beauty of the created universe. But almost immediately, the relationship was breached, and from that moment, reconciliation became both the root and the flower of authentic religion.

What precisely is the relationship which God first initiated and which because of human sin must be restored? What is it about God's relationship with humankind that makes the preservation of that relationship or reconciliation integral to human growth and fulfillment? According to the scriptural authors, the relationship of a human person to the creator consists in coming *to know* God. In general, the concept of *knowledge* in the Hebrew Scriptures is quite unlike our modern notion of knowledge, which has been influenced in great part by Greek philosophy. Ordinarily, we think of knowledge as something which is grasped by reason. For example, a westerner says he/she knows a certain thing when: (1) he/she has analyzed it completely; (2) he/she is able to explain the factors which caused it; (3) he/she can place it within the context of his/her already-acquired knowledge.

In the Scriptures, however, knowledge is understood as an intimate *relationship* with *someone*, a relationship of communion. For this reason, the close relationship of a wife and husband is referred to in the scriptures as *knowing one another* (Genesis 4:1). Similarly, the relationship with or knowledge of God is described in terms of a marital bond, and this knowledge of God was called for by the prophets as the first requisite for life (Isaiah 1:3; Jeremiah 2:8, 4:22, 31:32; Hosea 2:20,22, 4:1, 5:4, 6:6).

As T. Vriezen has pointed out, no attempts are made in the Hebrew Scriptures to define knowledge of God in an ontological or philosophical manner. Knowing God doesn't merely mean having an idea or concept about

God's nature; it is rather a perception of the divine through God's revealed words and works and the intimate response of one's entire being to that perception. More than an intellectual exercise, knowledge of God embraces all of life. It is first of all the awareness of *being known*, i.e., of being loved by the infinite God. The psalmist has expressed this awareness very beautifully:

> Yahweh, you examine me and know me, it was you who created my inmost self; for all these mysteries I thank you: for the wonder of myself, for the wonder of your works. Such knowledge is beyond my under- standing, a height to which my mind cannot attain . . . (Psalm 139:1,13-14,6).

Knowing God is essentially a communion with God, which is professed by faith and expressed in loving obedi- ence (Deuteronomy 6) to God's will (Micah 6:8). Knowl- edge of God is the recognition of *God as God*, of God as the wholly transcendent and Holy Other; it is also an awareness of *self as creature*, needy and dependent upon God as the source of all life and goodness.

The prophet Isaiah expressed this awareness in very vivid terms:

> Yahweh, you are our God – we are the clay, you the potter. We are all the work of your hand . . . Is the potter not better than the clay? Can something that was made say of its maker, "He did not make me"? or a pot say of the potter, "He is a fool"? (Isaiah 64:8, 29:16).

But, as the Scriptures attest, humankind all too often loses sight of a true awareness of God and self. Knowl- edge of God is perverted, the relationship with God is breached, and the healing of reconciliation becomes nec- essary for life and for survival. But just as it is entirely

God's unique prerogative as creator to initiate a relationship with humankind, so also is the process of reconciliation entirely contingent upon his mercy and love. Without God's prior initiative, without his reaching out to created humanity, there would be no relationship; there could be no reconciliation.

Reflections

1. Which is easier: to be reconciled with God or with another human being? Why?

2. Explain what the scriptures mean by *knowledge* of God.

Chapter Two

A Reaching Out, A Drawing Near

All of us have, at one time or another, seen a Hollywood presentation or televised network portrayal of primitive religious rituals. Therefore the following scenario isn't hard to imagine: An aboriginal tribe, deep in the bush, has determined that they must have angered their gods because they have been afflicted with some calamity like war, plague, flood or famine. The chief calls his people together; he announces that he and the tribal elders have decided upon a means to avert the disaster which threatens their extinction. At dawn, a great fire will be built, and when the time seems right, a fitting sacrifice will be cast upon it. Among the ancient peoples, the types of sacrifices varied: the offering could have been anything from a choice animal to a prince or princess! It was believed that if the sacrifice proved pleasing to the gods, they would postpone for a time or perhaps even cancel the chaos they had plotted against humanity.

Obviously there is a profound difference between this imagined scenario and the religious rituals of our Hebrew ancestors in the faith. Whereas the aboriginal devotees believed themselves to be helpless human pawns who were prey to the whims of a pantheon of disinterested gods, the people of Israel were aware of a personal loving, provident God, who became personally involved in human history as a parent is involved with a child.

Whereas other ancient peoples preferred to keep a safe distance from what they perceived as capricious, competitive and unpredictable deities and geared their energies toward *appeasing* these gods, Israel was privileged to be invited to share in a relationship with the Creator of the Universe; the chosen people were taught to maintain that relationship not by *appeasement* but by atonement. Whereas other ancient peoples preferred to remain anonymous to their gods, the people of Israel longed to draw near to their God, to be named by God, to know the divine name, to come "eyebrow-to-eyebrow together" in deep union, i.e., to be reconciled with their God. While there is no specific word in Hebrew for the word *reconciliation*, the term which best describes this concept is *kippur* or "atone." Atonement is a word which readily defines itself; it means a process of becoming one with, or at-one-ment.

One of the earliest means whereby Israel sought to participate in this at-one-ment or reconciliation with God was the sacrificial cult. Sacrifices were characteristic of Israel's entire history, from its earliest beginnings (Genesis 8:20) through the patriarchal (Genesis 15:9) and Mosaic (Exodus 5:3) periods, through the times of the judges (Judges 20:26) and kings (1 Kings 8:64), and especially during the post-exilic age (Ezra 3:1-6).

In the book of Leviticus (1-7), readers will find a description of the various sacrifices of ancient Israel, as they were performed in the post-exilic temple. The most solemn of all sacrifices was the holocaust or burnt offering (*'olah*). The verbal root of this term means "to rise up"; it was

ATONEMENT IS A MEANS OF BECOMING AT-ONE WITH God.

thought that the burnt offering (either an unblemished male animal, dove or pigeon) made atonement for the one who offered it and, as the odor of the sacrifice *rose up* to praise and glorify God, the relationship between the offerer and God was maintained and strengthened (Leviticus 1:4).

Another type of sacrifice (Leviticus 3) was the communion sacrifice (*zebah shelamim*), also called "the peace offering." Part of the offering was burned on the altar for Yahweh, a portion was given to the priest, and the rest was retained by the offerer, who cooked and shared it with his family as a feast before the Lord. As the name indicates, the communion sacrifice was motivated by a desire for communal solidarity and oneness with the Lord.

A third class of offerings were the sacrifices of expiation. Both the sin offering (Leviticus 4:1-5:13, *hattat*) and the guilt offering (Leviticus 5:14-26: *asham*) involved the sacrifice of an animal and sprinkling of its blood on the altar, as a sign of the sinner's desire to restore the relationship with God that had been weakened by human sin. This sacrifice was celebrated in a special and solemn manner on the annual Day of Atonement. With the high priest officiating, the entire nation of Israel participated in this ritual of reconciliation. Not a magical or superstitious means of appeasement, Israel's sacrificial liturgy was understood to be *God's gift*. "For the life of the flesh is in the blood; and I have given it to you upon the altar to make atonement for your sins" (Leviticus 17:11). The only guarantee that these efforts at reconciliation would be effective lay in Yahweh alone. In fact, as J. Bauer has noted, "It is precisely the recognition of the fact that *God* has opened up this possibility which makes the sacrificial act what it is."

If reconciliation with God were a mere human invention, it would be futile and ineffective. But, as is revealed in the Hebrew Scriptures, the opportunity for humankind to come "eyebrow-to-eyebrow together again with God" was made available by God, who never ceased to be present and never withheld a merciful pardon.

> WiтHouт тHε iNTεQRATioN of iNTεRioR moтiVATioN ANd εXTERNAL RiTUAL, woRsHip is εmPTY.

God was continually manifested as a God of tenderness and compassion (Exodus 34:6), who did not wish to respond in righteous and justifiable anger (Psalms 85:4, 103:8-12) but spoke peace to the people (Psalm 85:9).

By means of the sacrificial cult, Israel expressed its readiness for God's peace and signaled its gratitude for reconciliation. Each of the *external* rites was intended to express and make visible an *internal* sentiment. For example, the holocaust enunciated Israel's praise for and acknowledgment of Yahweh's greatness; the communion sacrifice illustrated a *desire for union,* and the expiatory rites voiced Israel's *admission of guilt* and *need for pardon.*

Without the integration of interior motivation and external ritual, the cult would degenerate into an empty sham. That this deterioration occurred in Israel's liturgy is evident in the scriptures, especially in the works of the prophets, who continually called their contemporaries to faith, conversion and honest, sincere worship.

Reflections

1. What are the various types of sacrifice in the Hebrew Scriptures?
2. What was the purpose of each of these sacrifices?
3. Why are such sacrifices no longer offered?

Chapter Three

How Do We Respond to God's Gift?

About fifteen centuries ago, a bishop from the diocese of Hippo in Northern Africa commented on the absolute necessity of reconciliation with God for human fulfillment. St. Augustine put it this way, "Lord, you have made us for yourself and our hearts are restless until they rest in you." In the first two chapters of this series, I have attempted to underscore the fact that "coming to rest in God" or reconciliation is a necessary aspect of Christian spirituality, as well as the fact that this drawing near is made possible only because our gracious and giving God has made it so. However, just because God is the principal author and initiator of this reconciliation, this does not preclude the necessary role of each human person. Reconciliation isn't simply a warm security blanket dropped onto a world of sleepy Linuses. As a gift of God, the invitation to "come eyebrow-to-eyebrow together again" with God is a challenge which summons those who would receive it to: actively cooperate with its graces, respond fully and in faith, i.e., with heart, hands and head, to all God offers,

> **Reconciliation isn't a warm security blanket, dropped onto a world of sleepy Linuses.**

and translate that active response to God into service and communal caring. Only then will reconciliation be an efficacious and fulfilling process of drawing near to the God who forgives, heals and gives rest.

Throughout the Hebrew and Christian Scriptures, the inspired authors set forth those conditions necessary for becoming one with or drawing near to God. In the first place, the process of reconciliation requires that the believer deliberately and purposefully *seek* God. In the eighth century B.C.E., the prophet Hosea (Hosea 10:12) advised his contemporaries: "Sow integrity for yourselves, reap a harvest of kindness, break up your fallow ground; it is time to go seeking Yahweh until he comes to rain salvation on you." Amos (Amos 4:4,6), a contemporary of Hosea, expressed a similar challenge, "Seek Yahweh and you shall live." Two centuries later, Deutero-Isaiah (Isaiah 55:6) exhorted his contemporaries in exile to "Seek, while Yahweh is still to be found; call, while Yahweh is still near!" That this seeking was not to be a vain effort is evident in the story of human salvation, wherein God remains constantly and readily available to the avid and sincere seeker (Wisdom 6:13).

Another condition required for "coming eyebrow-to-eyebrow with God" is an attitude of humility. Humility, derived from the Latin *humus*, meaning earth or soil, implies a radical truthfulness, a down-to-earthness which recognizes self as creature and as sinner. As Johannes Bauer has noted, this admission of guilt and the confession of sin are absolutely necessary preconditions for reconciliation with God, whether on the part of the individual (2 Samuel 12:13) or the community (1 Samuel 7:6). Sometimes this confession may be induced by serious illness (Psalms 2, 32, 38) or by some other source of suffering

(2 Samuel 24:17). Nevertheless, this moment of truth is necessary before reconciliation becomes possible.

For many believers, this moment of earthly humility occurs daily – perhaps even many times a day. Integral to this attitude of humility is a desire for conversion and a firm resolve to improve the quality of one's life and of one's response to God. Whenever the people were tempted to take a "shortcut" in the process of being reconciled to God, viz., by not complementing *external* ritual with an *interior* change of heart and mind, the prophets drew them up short.

Religious ritual, no matter how well-performed, no matter how costly, no matter how well accompanied by music and expressed in song, cannot take the place of a sincere heart, seeking to know God, eager to serve, and willing to translate that love and knowledge of God into love, knowledge and service of neighbor. Israel learned the hard lesson that no one could "come eyebrow-to-eyebrow together with God" without first "coming eyebrow-to-eyebrow together" with one's brothers and sisters in the Lord. Railing against the empty sham of purely external rituals, Isaiah spoke for God:

> What are your endless sacrifices to me, I am sick of holocausts of rams and the fat of calves . . . the smoke of your worthless offerings fills me with disgust . . . when you stretch out your hands and multiply your prayers, I turn my eyes away . . . Instead, learn to do good, search for justice, help the oppressed, be just to the orphan, plead for the widow. (Isaiah 1:11-17) Amos (5:21), Hosea (6:4-6) and Jeremiah (14:12) similarly exhorted their contemporaries.

Occasionally, Israel took desperate measures in its attempts to be reconciled with God. One very ancient ritual is detailed in the book of Leviticus (16:20-22). As part of the Yom Kippur or Day of Atonement liturgy, two goats were chosen from the herd. One goat was offered in sacrifice for the sins of the community; the other became the symbolic bearer of the people's guilt. Imposing hands on the goat, the priest confessed the people's sins; it was thought that this brought about a transmission of sins to the goat. Then the goat was sent forth (*caper emissarius* or scapegoat) from the community, carrying its evil burden out into the desert.

This primitive and superstitious notion was later followed by the aberration of child sacrifice. Although the story of Isaac (Genesis 22:1-19) was intended as a polemic against this practice, nevertheless there were instances in Israel's history wherein the people resorted to the sin of human sacrifice in a desperate attempt at reconciliation with God (2 Kings 23:10, Jeremiah 32:35, 2 Kings 21:6). Following the pagan rituals of their neighbors, some Israelite kings sacrificed their sons by fire to the god Molech.

In what is perhaps the most exquisite and most profound summary of true religion, the eighth-century prophet Micah reminded his people, and *all* believers, of the conditions necessary for coming eyebrow-to-eyebrow together again with God in reconciliation: When Israel asked:

> Act justly, love tenderly, walk humbly with your God.

With what gift shall I come into Yahweh's presence? . . . Shall I come with holocausts, with calves one-year-old? Will God be pleased with rams by the thousand, with libations of oil in torrents? Must I give my first-born for what I have done wrong, the fruit of my body for my own sin?

Yahweh answered:

What is good has been explained to you – this is what Yahweh asks of you, only this: to act justly, to love tenderly and to walk humbly with your God. (Micah 6:6-8)

Reflections

1. As a gift from God, reconciliation challenges the believer to: a. _____
   b. _____
   c. _____

2. What is humility and why is it essential for reconciliation?

CHAPTER FOUR

His Name Is Jesus

An old Russian proverb states: "God goes out to meet those who come to meet him." As any believer can attest, the truth of this ancient maxim is borne out in page after page of both our Hebrew and Christian Scriptures. For those who would meet and come "eyebrow-to-eyebrow together again with God," all that is necessary is to take the first step in movement toward God. The reconciling power of God does the rest; the sinner is welcomed and loved, embraced and graced with healing by the God for whom and by whom he/she was created.

In the Hebrew Scriptures, God was made manifest to those who came searching, and was encountered first through intermediaries. For example, when Abimelech lost favor with God, Abraham interceded on his behalf. Having heard Abraham's prayer, God healed and restored Abimelech (Genesis 20:17). Similarly, Moses acted as an intermediary to reconcile Pharaoh (Exodus 9:27,33), Miriam (Numbers 12:13ff) and Israel (Numbers 21:6-9)

> In the process of reconciliation, God goes more than halfway to meet those who seek mercy and forgiveness.

when each had fallen from favor. So too, Joshua, Samuel, and the prophets and priests of Israel acted as God's mediators of reconciliation. But in all of the Hebrew Testament, the most impressive figure to mediate the reconciling power of God was the Servant featured in the Songs of Deutero-Isaiah (42:1-9, 49:1-6, 50:4-11, 52:13-53:12).

Anointed and spirited by God, the Servant was to gather the people together (49:5), to teach them (50:4-10), to bear patient and humble witness to the truth (50:6, 53:7). His mediation on behalf of sinful people would go as far as the giving of his own life for their sakes (53:4-10). Because of the Servant's innocent suffering and death, sinners of all nations would be justified (53:8,11) and reconciled once again with God.

Some scholars have proposed that the prophet saw his own vocation or that of one of his contemporary colleagues (Jeremiah?) in terms of the Servant's reconciling ministry; others believe that Israel was to assume this role as its own. However, it wasn't until the coming of Jesus that the promised mission of the servant was fully realized and accomplished.

Indications that Jesus and the early Church consciously identified his saving work with that of the reconciling, suffering servant can be found in the gospels. While his contemporaries ascribed to messianic hopes in royal and material terms, and envisioned the messianic reign as the temporal and political dominion of Israel, Jesus identified his reign with service. He reached out to the poor, the unclean, the sinners, and embraced earthly suffering and death so that *all people* might enjoy eternal life (Luke 4:18ff, Mark 10:43ff, Matthew 20:26ff).

The reconciling power of Jesus' ministry has been portrayed very vividly in the Synoptic accounts of Jesus'

> **IN CHRIST JESUS, ALL OF HUMANKIND IS RECONCILED TO GOD, AND TO EACH OTHER.**

death on the cross. With the disarmingly simple statement, "And the veil of the temple was torn in two from top to bottom" (Matthew 27:51, Mark 15:37), the evangelists gave a graphic and eloquent summary of the theology of atonement or reconciliation. Recall that in Israel's temple, a veil was hung in front of the Holy of Holies (Exodus 26:31ff), thus separating this most sacred site of God's presence from the people. Only the high priest, and then only once a year did anyone draw near to Yahweh in this holy place. But Jesus changed all that. As the torn curtain in the passion narrative signified, Jesus' saving death forever removed the barriers which alienated humankind from God, viz., the barriers created by sin, externalism, empty cult, etc. Because of Jesus' words and works, and by virtue of his death and rising, all who believe are free to *draw near* . . . to be *reconciled* and healed, to "come eyebrow-to-eyebrow together again with God."

More than any other New Testament author, Paul is responsible for our understanding of all that Jesus' reconciling mission has accomplished. Aware that believers owe the gift and grace of reconciliation to God alone, the apostle wrote to the Corinthians, "All things are from God, to whom we are reconciled through Christ Jesus" (2 Corinthians 5:18). That no one could *merit* this gift, Paul reminded the church in Rome, "God's love for us is proven in that while we were still sinners Christ died for us. Indeed, while we were enemies, we were reconciled to God through the death of the Son" (Romans 5:8, 10).

Describing Jesus' unique and definitive role, the author of 1 Timothy declared, "For there is only one God and there is only *one mediator* between God and humanity, himself a man Christ Jesus, who sacrificed himself as our reconciliation" (1 Timothy 2:5).

The early Church also understood that the mysterious process of reconciliation to God is inextricably bound up with (1) the mystery of Jesus' Cross:

> In Christ Jesus, you that used to be far away have been brought near by the blood of Christ. For he is the peace between us and has made the two into one and has broken down the barrier by destroying in his own person the hostility caused by the rules and decrees of the law . . . he restored peace through the cross and reconciled us with God. (Ephesians 2:13-16);

(2) with the mystery of God's love for us:

> God loved us with so much love that God was generous in mercy; when we were dead through our sins, God brought us to life with Christ; it is through grace that we have been reconciled and raised up. (Ephesians 2:4-5)

There is a sort of divine irony in the fact that Paul, who had labored so diligently and ruthlessly to eradicate the followers of Jesus from the Hebrew community, and who regarded Jesus' influence upon Judaism as harmful and heretical, was also the one who would become an ardent missionary of Christ's reconciliation to the world.

Paul's conversion to Christ, i.e., his experience of God's reconciling power, impelled him to extol that power to others. Included in the Pauline (albeit disputed) corpus of literature is the following proclamation of the power of reconciliation: "God wanted all perfection to be found in

Christ and all things to be reconciled through him and for him, everything in heaven and everything on earth – when he made peace by his death on the cross" (Colossians 1:20).

Reflections

1. How did the character and activity of the suffering servant compare with the character and activity of Jesus?

2. How does Paul remind us that reconciliation is an unmerited gift of God to sinners?

CHAPTER FIVE

A Cosmic and Continuous Phenomenon

Most of us appreciate the fact that Leo Tolstoy (1828-1910) was a Russian author and nobleman, whose excellent contributions to the literary world included the epic novels *War and Peace* and *Anna Karenina*. But few of us are aware of the man's profound Christian faith and zealous commitment to social reform. In an age when others strained against an authoritarian leadership and pushed for a violent political revolution, Tolstoy understood that true freedom can only be found in drawing near to God. In this regard he declared, "The meaning of human life is the establishment of the kingdom of God on earth. That requires that the egotistical, hateful and dictatorial things be replaced with a life of brotherhood, freedom and reason."

There is a sad but all too common irony in the fact that Tolstoy, a sincere advocate of the reconciling power and peace of Jesus, suffered for his beliefs. He spent the last ten years of his life in alienation; he was excommunicated from the Orthodox Church in 1901, disowned by his family and shunned by his friends. Like the Lord whom he followed as a loyal disciple, Leo Tolstoy accepted the hardships and trials which his commitment to God precipitated; thereby he turned his suffering into a redemptive force for the sake of his contemporaries. Because of Tolstoy and others like him, the Christian faith behind the iron curtain has never dimmed. Indeed it has

> God absorbed alienation in an act of identification with humankind.

flourished amid the harshest persecution and political censure; today Christianity in Russia is enjoying a long awaited breath of free air in the atmosphere fostered by *glasnost*.

But the survival of the Russian church and of the entire Christian church worldwide should be no surprise to modern believers. Our endurance, our very existence has been assured by the person and mission of Jesus, in whom we have passed from death to a life that never ends . . . in whom and by whom we are reconciled, i.e., made capable of "coming eyebrow-to-eyebrow together again with God." According to William Gentz, "God made peace with us by the self-gift of Christ; God absorbed human *alienation* in an act of *identification* (incarnation) and vicarious atonement."

However, as we learn from Paul's theology of reconciliation in the Christian Scriptures, it is not only sinners who benefit from the saving work of Jesus. In his early letters (2 Corinthians 5:19), Paul spoke of the reconciliation of the world chiefly in terms of sinful humanity, but in later letters traditionally ascribed to Paul (Colossians, Ephesians), his notion of reconciliation widened to cosmic proportions: "Because God wanted all perfection to be found in Christ and all things to be reconciled through Christ, everything in heaven and everything on earth" (Colossians 1:19-20). Just as the created world was affected by the alienation of humanity from God, so too all of creation shares in the oneness with God effected by Christ:

Creation retains the hope of being freed, like us, from its slavery to decadence, to enjoy the same freedom and glory as the children of God. From the beginning until now the entire creation as we know has been groaning in one great act of giving birth; and not only creation, but all of us who possess the first fruits of the Spirit . . . (Romans 8:21-23)

Centuries before Paul, the inspired authors of the Hebrew Scriptures had expressed a similar awareness. Whereas before its fall from grace humanity enjoyed a harmonious relationship with all of the created universe, after the alienation wrought by

> **HUMANITY'S RECONCILIATION WITH God IS REFLECTED IN ALL THE CREATED UNIVERSE.**

sin, humanity experienced fear and estrangement in an often hostile and chaotic world. Similarly, when the prophets described Israel's redemption from sin, they indicated that humanity's reconciliation with God was to be reflected in the material universe as well: *Then shall the wolf live with the lamb, the panther shall lie down with the kid . . . the infant will play over the cobra hole . . . I will make rivers on barren heights, fountains in the midst of valleys, turn the wilderness into lake, plant trees in the desert . . . mountains and hills will break into joyful cries before you and all the trees of the countryside clap their hands. Cypress will grow, not thorns; crepe myrtle instead of briars . . .* (Isaiah 11:6-8, 41:18-19, 55:12-13).

In addition to the quelling of hostility between humanity and the created universe, the reconciling power of

Jesus' cross has also effected a harmony within and among all the peoples of the earth. When Christ became "our peace" (Ephesians 2), he worked to put an end to hatred and division and to integrate all the redeemed in faith and in love: "For he is the peace between us; he has made Jews and pagans one by breaking down the barriers that kept us apart . . . this was to create a new being in himself out of the two of them by restoring peace through the cross, to unite them in a single body and reconcile them with God" (Ephesians 2:14-15). Because of Christ, all believers are to consider themselves no longer in terms of race, heritage, sex or other social status; these are barriers which alienate and divide. Rather, those who accept Christ are challenged to think of themselves solely in terms of their reconciliation to God in Christ. Because of the relationship extended to each of us by God, we are consequently and definitively also related to one another.

The early Church wrote frequently and eloquently of this relationship: "So you are no longer aliens or foreign visitors; you are *citizens* like all the saints and *part of God's household*. You are *part of a building* that has the apostles and prophets for a foundation and Christ Jesus himself for its main cornerstone" (Ephesians 2:19-20). In further affirmation of this union, Paul explained that just as a human body, though it is made up of many parts, is a single unit, all of these parts, though many, make one body; so it is with Christ (1 Corinthians 12:12). While he acknowledged the dual effects of Christ's saving work, viz., reconciliation with God and reconciliation with all other members of the human family, Paul was also cognizant of the fact that believers are faced with the daily challenge of appropriating these graces for themselves.

Reflections

1. How should the peace and reconciliation effected by Jesus be reflected in the community of humankind?

2. What are some scriptural metaphors for the relationship that should bind us together?

3. Can you think of any other metaphors?

4. Which appeals to you most?

Chapter Six

God's Gift — Our Mission

In the course of this consideration of reconciliation, it has been established: (1) that reconciliation is a gratuitous gift of a loving God to an alienated and sinful people; (2) that reconciliation is the name given to the saving ministry of Jesus; (3) that because of Jesus, every barrier has been broken, every believer has been freed from the burden of sin and enabled to "draw eyebrow-to-eyebrow together again with God"; and (4) that the effects of this reconciliation are universal and cosmic, i.e., all of creation experiences and rejoices in humanity's nearness to God. At this juncture, attention will be focused on the *means* whereby believers continue to participate in the process of reconciliation, the sacraments.

Each of the sacraments is an event of grace whereby the believer encounters Christ. Vatican Council II affirmed the importance of the sacraments in this way: "The purpose of the sacraments is to sanctify people, to build up the body of Christ and to give worship to God. Because they are signs, they also instruct. They not only presuppose faith but they also nourish, strengthen and express it" (*Constitution on Sacred Liturgy*, No. 59).

Centuries ago St. Ambrose declared: "You have shown yourself to me, face to face, O Lord, for it is you that I find in your sacraments." By virtue of the sacramental encounter, the believer is joined intimately and really with the saving activity of Jesus' dying and rising. As a result, and by cooperation with God's grace, every sacramental experience should effect within the believer a change for the better. This change or conversion is part of the lifelong process of reconciliation, of drawing near to God in Christ.

In Baptism, believers are initiated into the life and body of Christ by being reconciled to God and to one another within the human community. But baptismal initiation is precisely that – a *beginning*. Baptism isn't a *permanent* guarantee of faith or forgiveness; each day, the believer's baptismal commitment must be affirmed by a *daily* cooperation with God's grace. Only by embracing the task of *continual* reconversion or reconciliation can one remain firm in his/her baptismal commitment. Two of the central means by which Christians can renew the graces of their baptism are the sacraments of Penance (or Reconciliation) and the Eucharist.

In the gospel according to John, Jesus is portrayed as commissioning his disciples for a ministry of forgiveness: "Peace be with you, as God has sent me, so I send you . . . Receive the Holy Spirit. If you forgive anyone's sins, they are forgiven them; if you hold them bound, they are held bound" (John 20:21-23). Based on this mandate, the Church has continued to exercise Jesus' mission of forgiveness.

Specifically, the sacrament of Reconciliation affords repentant sinners the

> THERE CAN bE NO limiT TO THE OVERTURES of RECONCiliATiON which bELiEVERS MAKE TOWARd ONE ANOTHER.

grace of drawing near again to God. As the believer acknowledges and confesses personal sin, he/she is not only reunited with God but is also reconciled with other believers. But just as Christ is the sacrament or sign of God's reconciling love, so also must forgiven Christians be sacraments or signs of Christ's reconciling power for one another. This fact has been made very clear in the gospels: Peter, thinking he was being quite magnanimous, asked of Jesus, "Lord, when someone wrongs me, shall I forgive him seven times?" (Matthew 18:21) Seven was considered by Israelites to be the symbol of fullness, a perfect number. Jesus' answer to Peter, " . . . not seven times but seventy times seven times" (Matthew 18:22), stretched that number unto infinity. For believers in Jesus, *no limit* can be placed on the overtures of reconciliation we are to make toward one another!

> Those freed from sin by reconciliation are thereby called to free others.

Similarly, we learn from the gospels that no one can expect to come "eyebrow-to-eyebrow together again" with God unless he/she is also willing to do the same with all others in the human community. In teaching his followers to pray, Jesus counseled that they ask God: to "forgive us our trespasses as we forgive those who trespass against us." In other words, believers should pledge their willingness to be reconciled with one another in the same breath that they ask for God to extend that same grace of reconciliation to them.

Also underscored in the gospels is the notion that without forgiveness or reconciliation between members of the community there can be no true prayer, no true communion with God: "If you bring your gift to the altar and recall that someone has anything against you, leave your gift at the altar, go first to be reconciled to your brother and/or sister, and then come and offer your gift" (Matthew 5:23-24). A very striking point with regard to this text is frequently overlooked. Notice that the passage states: "If you recall that someone has anything against you . . . " The implication seems to be not that *you* have wronged *another* but that *another person* has wronged *you*. That the first step toward reconciliation should be taken by the wronged party is one of the challenges of Christian discipleship. But it is precisely this largeness of heart which is a true reflection of God's love. At the same time, the willingness to take the first step toward reconciliation is an act which sanctifies and edifies the entire human family. As R.J. Novak has noted, "Reconciliation is not just a word or a Pavlovian stimulus producing whole sets of good acts. To be involved in reconciliation is to be a part of a tremendous act of faith that people will become different." To take the first step in the reconciliation process is an act of faith in God's power to enable others (and ourselves) to become better, to become beautifully transformed by God's grace.

Finally, it is by our participation in the Eucharist, or Lord's Supper, that believers most fully experience the powerful grace of reconciliation. In the reading of the sacred word and in the sharing of Jesus' Body and Blood, there is an encounter with the living God. God forgives and feeds us, God draws sinners near and urges them to draw near to one another. From that sacred encounter, the faithful are sent forth to be missionaries of God's love, messengers to the world that God invites each and all, to be reconciled . . . to "come eyebrow-to-eyebrow together again" with God. If all believers would only begin to seriously exercise their ministry of reconciliation . . . can you imagine what might happen to this world?

Reflections

1. How can a believer be a sacrament of reconciliation for others?

2. How is the Eucharist or Lord's Supper the fullest experience of the power of reconciliation?